Praise for People You Follow

This is Hayley in book  th her
humour giving a light t   'e one.
Beautifully written wor   sional
necessary cry.

           — KAIA GERBER, model and actress

Hayley's journey to find self-love is both heartbreaking and
humorous. I recognized my own younger self and how we, as
women, struggle to find our value through the eyes of others.
While Hayley's story may be more dramatic than others, we are
rooting for her as she finds herself and the power of "no."

           — CINDY CRAWFORD, model and actress

A good songwriter is someone who makes the listener feel like
the words were stolen right out of their mouth, and Hayley has
that same quality as an author. *People You Follow* left me feeling colourful, excited, empowered, completely vulnerable, a little
heartbroken, and incredibly inspired.

           — CHARLOTTE LAWRENCE, singer-songwriter and model

People You Follow is a fucked-up *Alice in Wonderland* journey down
the rabbit hole of L.A.'s most subtly toxic industry, and it's also
funny, brilliant, coy, playful, and wise. I feel so lucky that Hayley
is here to express how hard dating in Hollywood is for the bunch
of us, and I'm also glad that young women can read about her
emotional pratfalls and save themselves the same pain as they
work to become artists as skilled as she is.

           — LENA DUNHAM, author of *Not That Kind of Girl*

Hayley's memoir masquerades as a comedic take on a young woman discovering and defining her sexuality. You are so distracted by the breezy comedy of the insane true-life stories that you don't see the gut punches coming.

— BILL LAWRENCE, writer/creator of *Scrubs*,
Cougar Town, and *Spin City*

Reading Hayley Gene Penner's memoir felt like I was with my funniest, naughtiest friend, who came over to drink tequila and tell me secret stories. Each cautionary tale is full of dark humour, desire, and sexy sex in the most vulnerable and authentic way. I loved every minute.

— CHRISTA MILLER, actress and model

people you follow

people
you
follow

a memoir

hayley gene penner

DUNDURN
TORONTO

Publisher: Scott Fraser | Acquiring editor: Rachel Spence | Editor: Susan Fitzgerald
Cover designers: Danica Penner-Vargek, Laura Boyle
Cover illustration: Danica Penner-Vargek
Cover photographer: Kendra Penner
Printer: Marquis Book Printing Inc.

Library and Archives Canada Cataloguing in Publication

Title: People you follow: a memoir / Hayley Gene Penner.
Names: Penner, Hayley Gene, 1985- author
Identifiers: Canadiana (print) 20200196650 | Canadiana (ebook) 20200197541 | ISBN 9781459747142
  (softcover) | ISBN 9781459747159 (PDF) | ISBN 9781459747166 (EPUB)
Subjects: LCSH: Penner, Hayley Gene, 1985- | LCSH: Singers—Canada—Biography. | LCSH:
Composers— Canada—Biography.
Classification: LCC ML420.P413 A3 2020 | DDC 782.42164092—dc23

We acknowledge the support of the Canada Council for the Arts and the Ontario Arts Council for our publishing program. We also acknowledge the financial support of the Government of Ontario, through the Ontario Book Publishing Tax Credit and Ontario Creates, and the Government of Canada.

Care has been taken to trace the ownership of copyright material used in this book. The author and the publisher welcome any information enabling them to rectify any references or credits in subsequent editions.

The publisher is not responsible for websites or their content unless they are owned by the publisher.

Printed and bound in Canada.

VISIT US AT

dundurn.com | @dundurnpress | dundurnpress | dundurnpress

Dundurn
3 Church Street, Suite 500
Toronto, Ontario, Canada
M5E 1M2

For Lily, for later.

school lunch analogy

Anne Lamott asked me to talk about my packed school lunches. She, of course, doesn't realize she asked me, specifically, to do this. She asked all of us who read *Bird by Bird*. But since I am one of that "us," she did ask me.

Firstly, nothing was as good as no packed lunch at all. Nothing was as delicious as a crumpled ten-dollar bill passed back from the front seat of our grey Venture minivan, passed back with a look that said, "Don't get used to this. It's back to bag lunches tomorrow."

That crumpled ten-dollar bill meant fries dusted with neon-orange seasoning salt. That ten-dollar bill meant friends reaching over our paper plates. That ten-dollar bill meant power and popularity. That ten-dollar bill gave us a peek into adulthood and the first swells of pride surrounding money.

Some days my lunch was a true surprise, especially when I missed the opportunity to badger my parents for an extra package of Dunkaroos or Gushers, or when I was too busy upstairs trying to tame my hair or wish away a zit to bully them into making better choices while assembling my lunch.

In my memory, Dad made lunch. When he was home, and not on tour or shooting his TV show, I told people he was a professional grocery shopper. With most touring musicians, when they are home, they are really home, making up for the time their spouse was parenting alone by being a full-time child wrangler/taxi driver/dishwasher/driveway shoveller.

Perhaps the lunches my dad made stand out more because, the truth is, the lunches my mom made were merely good. They were consistent and generally unsurprising in a way that I found comforting. My dad's lunches, on the other hand, were like tying a frayed rope to your feet and leaping off a rickety bridge. The anticipation was always of impending doom, but every so often that rope would hold and the sun would set at the exact moment you began the free fall and a single tear would trickle down your cheek out of pure joy and euphoria. You'd open your lunch and there it would be, a straight-up Nutella sandwich.

That Nutella sandwich says so much to me now. That sandwich says that my dad was in a rush that morning. It says that he was too tired to care about pushing healthy options. It says that my mom was probably already at her studio by the time the lunches were being made or, even more likely, that my dad actually didn't make my lunch at all. It says that my mom did without my realizing it, and she made it because she knew I'd like it.

At that time, however, it only meant that my family really fucking loved me and that I was really fucking special. It only meant that, for thirty minutes over our lunch period, I could rejoice in the jealous faces of my peers trying not to stare as I took slow-motion bites. While they hung their heads in the aromatic shame of their egg salad sandwiches, I'd lean back in my chair and lick my lips, thinking, *I'm better than you.*

Then there were the days I was certain my parents must not want me to have friends. I'd fearfully open the unnervingly heavy, soft, soggy brown-paper bag and reach in with slow, steady precaution, half expecting something to bite my fingers off. One at a time, I'd grab hold of the three moist plastic bags and pull them out.

First, the carrots and raisins bag. Yes, carrots and raisins go together in carrot cake. They go together beautifully with sugar and flour and eggs and butter. However, if you put a handful of raisins in a Ziploc bag, then wash some carrots and toss them in, what you end up with is a bag of carrots in room-temperature raisin water.

Then there was the sandwich bag, holding tuna or egg salad. Releasing one of these from its airtight little bag meant notifying the entire cafeteria all at once, like pissing in one of those pools that turns urine bright pink, causing everyone to turn and stare and point and distance themselves.

What was even more fucked-up was how crazy delicious both of those sandwiches were. Shamefully delicious. But it was near-impossible to expose how much I loved those sandwiches. Revealing that you loved egg or tuna salad might as well be revealing that you had been masturbating with the shower head since you were thirteen — something every single human woman with a detachable shower head has done, even though most of us would like to pretend we haven't or don't or didn't, like, just a few hours ago.

The third Ziploc bag was a game of Russian roulette. It could hold anything from loose chocolate chips to a cut-up pear slathered with peanut butter. What was in this third bag usually depended on the time of year. If it was after Halloween, it could be a tiny box of Smarties or a mini Wunderbar or one little turd-shaped Bounty bar. If it was Easter, you could expect to find a few shards of the large chocolate egg that sat above the shelf at home (as if putting it up high would keep four teenage kids out of it). If it was Christmas, you might get a buttered piece of panettone or a sack of leftover roasted parsnips.

Lunches were a way to show the world who you were and what your home life looked like. Through a single meal, we were let into each other's lives outside of school. We were invited into each other's parental relationships — their financial stability, how strict they were, how busy they were — and we were able to quietly compare ourselves to each other, assigning value based on things outside of our control.

This book is my lunch.

This book is a lunch that I packed for myself but that hundreds of people helped me make.

This pungent egg salad is not meant to repulse or offend anyone. This burnt Michelina's microwave pizza was not burned intentionally to spite anyone or ruin their dining experience.

This lunch was prepared because, without realizing it, I had been starving until the moment I took my first bite.

In many ways, I didn't even know I had been pushing these things deep into an unnervingly heavy, soft, soggy brown-paper bag until the moment I started dumping them all out on a big circular wooden table in the middle of a cafeteria, until the moment I found myself standing on the table, naked over heaps of carrots in room-temperature raisin water, ankle-deep in mounds of loose chocolate chips and stale almonds, yelling, "This is my fucking lunch."

I am sure some of you will look at the pile beneath me and think what I am calling almonds are in fact grapes. Some of you will think what I see as burnt is in fact toasted.

And that's okay.

I have to be all right with losing some friends who may really hate egg salad. Friends who don't think it's egg salad at all and are furious at me for calling it that, or, perhaps even worse, friends who helped me make these sandwiches and felt certain I'd never feel like sharing them.

The point of this book is to look at myself in the mirror and say out loud, "I really like egg salad."

This book is about being brutally honest with you and with myself.

So, have some if you want. Or don't if you don't. Grab one of my mushy sandwiches and hurl it at the wall if it makes you feel better.

But I am sharing this because I have to.

I'm sharing because my brown-paper bag runneth over, and I need to make room for the rest of my life's lunches.

tal

his hand and her head

I've watched this video dozens of times. It's only thirteen seconds long.

Its thumbnail is an out-of-focus shot of Tal's off-white carpet. Off-white from shoes and guitar cases and the passing of vacuum-free time.

I press play and the still, blurry carpet clicks into motion. The camera pans to reveal a mattress on a plain metal bed frame. The frame has wheels, though there's no chance of it sliding anywhere. It sinks closer to the hardwood under the crusty carpet to the rhythm of deep male grunts and muffled female gasps.

The shot skims by a bright-pink suitcase pressed against a full wall of mirrors. In the mirror we see Tal pushing himself into the lily-white ass of a faceless woman.

I know she is me because I recognize the sound of her voice. I know the curve of her back. Her hair is shoulder length, and I remember when she got that manicure.

With his free left hand, Tal pushes her head down, her face pressed into the sheets. With the other, he quietly films them.

Though not them.

Not really.

He's filming himself.

I've watched this video dozens of times. It's only thirteen seconds long.

I used to watch it to admire the curve of her back, the length of her neck. To watch her being devoured. I used to watch it as the absolute proof that she was desirable.

But it looks different this time. I am not focused on the curve of her back or the length of her neck. I am focused on his left hand. I am focused on his left palm using her head to prop himself up in order to film his performance.

And I'm suddenly back in that moment. And I'm blinded by the mask of sheets he's made me. And I am nowhere. I feel him pushing into me from behind as the small patch of sheets under my mouth becomes damp and warm.

He'll finish in a second. He'll pull himself out of me and walk into the bathroom. I'll know he's done by my sudden aloneness. I'll turn my head in time to see him peek back into the room, throw a hand towel in my direction. I'll hear him run a shower.

I'll awkwardly reach behind me and wipe his cum off my back. I'll reach farther down and collect any remaining mess from between my thighs.

I'll grab the warm sheets, pull them around my body, and sit up to look at myself in the mirror, and there will be two of me.

The me in the moment. The me who is suddenly small. The me who suddenly remembers being carried up the stairs by her dad after falling asleep in the living room. The me who remembers the smell of his flannel shirts and the total safety of the left side of his chest.

Then the me in the mirror. The me who is almost proud of her debauchery. The me who is quietly whispering, "Look, we did turn out to be fuckable. This is what we wanted, right?"

tobias

a long arm reaches

"Please don't sign that publishing deal," Tobias said from the driver's seat of his parents' grey Acura.

I had just gotten back to Toronto after spending six months in England trying to outrun my broken heart. In my experience, nothing kick-starts personal growth like soul-shattering rejection. Ben. Sigh. Ben ripped my heart out like prematurely removing the staples from a bullet wound. I had only just started to trust that he, the staples, would keep me together, protecting me from infection or from a rogue Junior Mint falling into the hole.

I hate the word *dump*. It's so violent and uneven and unkind. It brings me back to the bear-infested dump at our cabin or the act of scraping a leftover chicken carcass into the trash. It's a terrible word, and it's exactly what happened. Being dumped by Ben lit a tiny flame, a flickering blue light at the end of a long grey wick attached to a cold steel cannon. A cannon that shot me over the pond to write restaurant reviews for a food magazine and to try my hand at songwriting with some friends of friends.

I ate and cried and wrote, then ate and cried and wrote some more. I bought a brand-new Moleskine and an overpriced pen and laid them officially beside my perfectly aligned silverware, trying to fool the restaurant staff into thinking I had any right to, arguably, the best job in the world.

Page one of my notebook read, *We popped the rich snails into our mouths, relishing the expert balance of earthy and indulgent. For our main courses we had roasted suckling pig belly with cep polenta and garlic sauce and a halibut special with yellow zucchini, mussels, and a seafood sauce.*

Page two read, *I don't understand. We were happy a fucking month ago. I feel like my chest is caving in all the time. How do you just stop loving a person? He's my person. What do I even do now? He's ruined so many of my favourite songs and movies and smells and outfits and street corners and he's gonna shake out of this. He has to.*

These journal entries morphed into music. I sat on the London Eye and watched the city rise and fall beneath me, then dragged my emotional baggage into every songwriting session — where emotional baggage is absolutely encouraged. At the end of my trip, I headed back to Toronto with nearly twenty songs about my sweet, sad, bleeding heart.

When I got back from London, I thought I would take my collection of songs and see if I could land myself a publishing deal. I thought I would try to get a big company to give me money to write songs in exchange for half the ownership. I sent at least fifty cold emails to at least fifty publishing companies and got only one email back, a substantial Canadian company offering me the worst deal of all time. A deal that, at the time, I thought was the best thing that had ever happened to me. *What?! You wanna give me ten thousand dollars to own my fucking soul forever? Where do I sign?* At a certain point, you're so excited to be offered anything that you lose any instinct to investigate what, precisely, is in that outstretched hand. Ten thousand dollars might as well have been ten million.

As I was getting acquainted with the company, Tobias, a young manager, randomly reached out to the same company in the hopes of finding a new female singer–songwriter to manage. They passed my info to Tobias. One thing led to another, until there I was, in Tobias's parents' Acura.

"Seriously, though, please don't sign that publishing deal," said Tobias, as he turned into the driveway of the house of a producer I'd never met before. He parked the car and continued his pep talk as we walked into the home together. "My brother, Tal, is a big songwriter in L.A. Just give me a couple weeks before you decide whether you're gonna sign that deal or not. I'm gonna keep putting you in writing sessions with some dope producers here, then we'll send my brother some of your stuff, and if he likes it, we'll bring you out to L.A. to see if you guys get on in person."

In every way, Tobias was my saviour. As soon as we started working together, he started filling my schedule with incredible writers and producers, many of whom I'm still close with now. He came to sessions all over Toronto with me and cheered me on from recording-studio couches. He nurtured my relationship with songwriting and made me believe in myself, while seamlessly redefining what Toronto meant to me. He transformed the city from one giant reminder of my relationship with Ben to this filthy yet fertile ground for my blossoming ambition.

Then finally, one cold November day, Tobias sent one of my songs to Tal for a critique. And Tal loved it. He loved it so much that he offered to fly me to Los Angeles and put me up for a month or so to see how I got on with the rest of his small production team. To see if we had chemistry and if I would perhaps want to stay in L.A. indefinitely and sign a deal directly to him.

I'd seen the 1998 Gwyneth Paltrow classic *Sliding Doors*, so I was hyperaware of the different paths that can unfold when you do or do not catch the train. When a seemingly inconsequential opportunity is missed or taken. This was me catching the train, which in my case was a plane. This was me stepping into a pivotal and perfectly orchestrated sequence of events, recognizable only in hindsight.

tal

drinking the kool-aid

A couple weeks before I moved to Los Angeles, I found a drawing I'd made when I was six. It was at the bottom of a box labelled *Goodwill?* The unintentionally abstract illustration shows a long, sparkling, red convertible, with a somehow dripping Hollywood sign in the distance. A tall, dangerously thin, flowing-haired young woman leans against the shimmering hood, her hand holding a cellphone to her ear. At the top of the crumpled piece of construction paper I'd written *Hayley, 21-years-old.*

I turned twenty-six a few weeks before coming to L.A.

I definitely did not have a convertible; I tossed a Honda Civic rental onto my buckling Visa. And my cellphone barely worked in the U.S.

I had been in L.A. for forty-four days. Tal's company put me up in a sketchy basement apartment. If I hadn't been living underground, I bet I would have been able to see the Hollywood sign from my window.

I pushed all the cheap furniture up against the poorly painted walls in the living room and devoted two hours every morning to P90X. I was determined to at least appear as though I'd made it, and that started with a rigorous workout regimen. My goal was to have at least a few people say they were worried about me when I went home to Winnipeg for Christmas.

Tal was this charming, vibrant, extraordinary writer. He almost instantly became my new favourite person. He was funny and tall and dark and took up all the space in every room, and I was convinced that if he thought I could make it, I could.

My first two months in L.A. consisted of driving to the studio every morning at 8:00 a.m. and spending four hours alone in Tal's vocal booth before getting booted into the tiny, fluorescent-lit storage space in the back of the building. I would sit at a desk that was dwarfed by a horrendous neon mural and wait for him to pop his head out of his room, perhaps offering me an opportunity to write something with him.

It felt like a sort of long-winded audition, and I thought I was doing well. He would dip into my little incubator every few hours to see if I'd written a hit or to say, "Come on. We're walking to the grocery store."

He made me laugh on the way while casually lecturing me about songwriting and the industry and who to trust. Then he'd buy a watermelon, a pound of cold cuts, and a bag of almonds and we would walk back together. And he trusted me. He told me about the two women he was in love with, how deeply he loved them both, how he didn't know what to do. They didn't know about each other, but that didn't make me think less of him. I felt welcomed into his inner circle. I felt like his confidant and friend. I saw him as a struggling man and I was glad he had me to talk to.

We would drop the food in the fridge, then we'd head outside, where I'd watch him play basketball alone with his shirt off for half an hour before we got back to work.

He had a two-bedroom apartment in North Hollywood and decided to rescue me from the Hollywood basement he'd put me in. I thought living with him would be fun. I'd get rid of my rental car and commute to the studio with him. He understood that I didn't have money and couldn't really make any, since I was officially a tourist, so he'd feed me and take care of me in a way that made me feel like I'd found a little home.

At the studio, I spent a lot of time in the bathroom. I didn't need to use it. I just didn't really feel like writing. I'd go and look in the mirror for ten or fifteen seconds, decide whether I loved or hated my body that day, then flush the toilet with nothing in it, run the tap to suggest I was washing my hands, and walk out. Maybe take an ass selfie for whatever guy was getting my ass selfies at that time. I somehow felt that by taking multiple bathroom breaks, I would at least seem productive. Like these pee breaks were the result of hard work and perseverance.

One morning of a long weekend, when most of the producers were with their families, it was just the two of us in the building. I came out of the bathroom and looked for Tal. He wasn't in the common room or shoving cold cuts into his mouth in the kitchen. There was almost no noise coming out of his studio room, so I knocked without expectation.

He said, "Come in. I wanna play you a new song." He opened his computer. I paused in embarrassment for him. On the screen a girl with long black hair was getting fucked from behind while she sucked off some Tarzan-looking dude in front of her.

Tal left the screen open long enough for the man in her mouth to finish on her rosy-pink cheeks and lips, sealing her eyes shut like he was planning on making her a papier-mâché mask. Then he said, "Oh shit. That's embarrassing," and closed his computer.

He pulled out a guitar to play the song live. He sang with his whole heart, all emotional and generous with the intimacy of his performance. It felt like an invitation into his private self.

We just sort of casually moved past the accidental porn mishap, though I guess I suddenly knew what he liked. And suddenly he knew that I knew what he liked. It felt like this weird shared moment actually brought us closer. Like walking in on somebody masturbating. You can't unsee it — you can only decide together to pretend like you didn't or, at the very least, pretend it didn't leave a totally indelible imprint.

He took me for Korean barbecue, then moved me into his apartment.

françois

the virgin

Throwing me a quick glance, then immediately securing his gaze on the steering wheel, François said, "I was gonna come to the door. Fuck, you're really pretty."

"Well, I'm sorry. I can go back in if you wanna try it again."

He smiled and looked at me out of the corner of his eye before pulling away from Tal's typical, piss-coloured North Hollywood complex, which I had just moved into.

He was adorably nervous. I don't generally find nervousness sexy, but there is something about it that can make you feel comfortable and safe on a first date.

We pulled up to the charming little restaurant. He told me to remain seated as he parked, and then he walked around the car and opened my door. That kind of chivalry is not important to me, but when it comes unexpectedly, it can make me feel powerful and emotionally unavailable in a warm, cozy, protected way.

We shared a number of dishes under a canopy of Christmas lights on the snug patio, learning bits about each other the way you do on a first date. François had gone to all-boys schools his entire life, then moved to L.A. when he was eighteen to work at the studio, where I met him. This history of back-to-back boys' clubs perfectly put into context his entire demeanour and how dazzled he was by my perceived beauty.

He slurped pad Thai noodles as I talked about a few exes, at which point he accidentally told me he was a virgin. This information did not come up as an offering; rather, it bubbled to the surface like oil in water, separating and revealing itself unintentionally.

"I get to be your first?" I blurted out.

He blushed hard, like some three-handed demon had slapped both his cheeks and his forehead at the exact same time.

We finished our meal, and as we started walking over to his car, François said, "So, I have a few possible activities for tonight, if that's okay with you." He led me around the back of his car, pausing at the rear bumper.

"Is one of the activities you clubbing me in the back of the head and tossing me in your trunk?"

He smiled awkwardly, then pressed a button on his key chain, popping open the trunk to reveal two things: a disposable camera and a can of spray paint. He pulled them out, shoved them into a black canvas bag, and said, "Let's go for a walk."

We started strolling down a back alley parallel to Melrose Avenue. We passed restaurant Dumpsters and delivery entrances.

François appeared to be looking for something, though it wasn't clear what. Head down, scanning the uneven pavement, he stopped on a smoothish chunk of grey cement, spotlit by a struggling street light. He reached into his bag, pulled out the spray paint, and motioned for me to step back.

Bending over, he began spraying:

(Shake shake shake) *H a y l e y* (shake shake shake) *C a n* (shake) *I k i s s* (shake shake) *y o u ?*

I smiled, imagining the moment he had decided to pull this move. Like, did he see it in a movie? Like, if I reached into his pocket, would the receipt for one can of spray paint still be in there?

I walked up to him, close enough to move in for a kiss, hovered for a moment, then took the can and motioned for him to back up.

(Shake shake shake) *U M M M M* (shake shake) ...
(shake) *Y E* (shake shake) *S.*

Smiling nervously, he walked over, leaned in, and kissed me. I felt his face flush against mine, the blood rushing to his cheeks and lips.

He stepped back, reached into his black canvas bag again, and pulled out the disposable camera. He climbed up the side of a Dumpster and reached his long arm up over his head to take a picture of our spray-painted exchange on the pavement. Then he jumped down, unintentionally gifting me a glimpse of his olive-toned abs on the way. His strong, spindly, licorice body landed in front of me and, riding on the momentum of the jump, he kissed me again.

A woman leaned over her balcony and started screaming at us for defacing her property. We scurried into the shadows like guilty raccoons.

It was his birthday a few nights later. Tal was out of town, so I decided to invite François over for some good ol'-fashioned deflowering. I thought it wise to buy a cake rather than make one, realizing I was in a particular position of power.

When the buzzer buzzed, I casually strolled to the front door of the building, giving him a couple extra minutes to sit in his pent-up anticipation. I opened the heavy beige door to find him wearing a navy-blue dress jacket and cradling a bouquet of flowers.

So cute. Just crazy cute.

I leaned over the flowers and kissed him tenderly, then took the vibrant bundle from his hands and led him toward the apartment.

We started making out in front of the long L-shaped couch in the living room. He bent me back over the cushions, my hands extending behind me to prop my ass up on the armrest. We sloppily made out like this for a few minutes, and then he pulled back and said, "I have a surprise for you … but you have to open my shirt to get it."

He inched me into the kitchen. Facing the clinical fluorescent stove light, I began unbuttoning his shirt cautiously. Written in dark-red ink across his left pectoral were the words *Though you may stray. You'll be here to stay.*

I searched for something to say. Something in support of his astonishingly bad idea. As I looked at his sweet, generous face, every stupid thing I had ever done in the name of love flashed before my eyes. I put my hand on his tender, swollen, freshly tattooed chest and said, "Thank you."

Then I inched him back to the living room and gave him his first blow job on Tal's couch.

tal

how it started

I pulled my yoga mat onto the living room floor in Tal's tiny, carpeted, piss-coloured North Hollywood apartment and sat with my legs extended in front of me. I bent forward, reaching for my toes, inhaling and exhaling as I pulsed with my hands against my calves.

Tal came out of his room to find me on my back in a fetal position, rolling out my spine. He grabbed a bottle of Evian water from his always-stocked fridge and sat on the couch in front of me. We talked as I finished up. He launched into one of his songwriting lessons, surprise-lecturing me the way he had been for the previous three months, explaining that he had solid evidence his new band was already better than Coldplay, though they had yet to release anything.

Then he said, "You've been working so hard. Come on, I'll give you a massage."

I exhaled. "Oh my god, I need one." I scooted my body over in front of the couch to lean against his legs.

As I was midscoot, he said, "No, come on, I'll give you a real massage." Still not entirely sure what he meant, I got up and followed him down the hall. "Go lay down," he told me. "I'm gonna grab some oil."

I walked into my dark, carpeted room, nervous and not sure how to say no to my boss who I really cared about, my boss who was housing me and feeding me and offering me an opportunity to stay in the country and a world of resources I had been fantasizing about for as long as I could remember fantasizing about anything. I walked into the dark, carpeted room, considering the timing of his sudden interest in the art of massage.

At that point, I wasn't even sure what exactly I would be saying no to. I lay down flat on my stomach. I was wearing shorts and a halter bodysuit that exposed my whole back. I listened to Tal puttering around the apartment while I waited quietly, my left cheek against the pillow.

When Tal first flew me to Los Angeles a few months earlier, he was in the midst of two relationships. He had been nurturing a long-distance, long-term relationship with Molly, a famous Canadian gymnast, and another with June, a young, creative, artsy wisp of a woman who lived around the corner from the studio. He was conflicted, quietly juggling the love of these two women, who knew nothing about each other. And he confided in me. I felt like a friend and non-judgmental confidant, while struggling with my own questions about moral obligation and where that line is for someone on the periphery. I spent a lot of time with June. The three of us would go to the beach on Saturdays, the Melrose Farmers' Market on Sundays. We sat in Tal's studio and listened to music and laughed and ate cold cuts out of a supermarket Ziploc bag. In a studio otherwise filled exclusively with men, she glowed like a lighthouse. We rolled our eyes at the same unfunny jokes and liked the same shows, and together we lobbied for Tal to not stay at the studio until two in the morning. She became a friend while I sat quietly on information I was well aware would break her heart.

Telling her never really felt like an option. Of course it was, but it didn't feel like that. Tal had sponsored my U.S. work permit and signed me to his production team in partnership with a major record label. I had just signed the paperwork, officially tethering me to him for three years at the very least. A tight leash from his hand to my throat.

So I was in some ways relieved when June and Molly found out about each other. June was looking through Tal's phone and found pictures of Molly. She found Molly's number and called. In a meeting of broken hearts, she introduced herself and imploded Tal's entire precarious operation, leaving him single for the first time in years while I did crunches in his spare bedroom.

I flipped my face from one side to the other, exposing my now pillow-creased cheek. Tal came back in the room and closed the door behind him. He climbed onto the bed and straddled me, sitting comfortably on my ass. Before opening the bottle of oil, he ran his hands up my back, grabbed the top of my bodysuit and pulled it over my head and down my chest so that I was fully naked from the waist up.

He uncapped the oil, flipped the bottle upside down, and poured some along my spine in one confident motion. Staring at the blue wall beside the bed, my cheek still on the pillow, I watched him shift on top of me out of the corner of my eye.

The warm oil dripped steadily down around my ribs as he pressed his palms deeper into my skin, inching his fingers under the top of my shorts. Realizing where this was heading, I abruptly said, "Well, that was great, thanks." I grabbed my halter strap and pulled it back over my head, casually bucking him off, then moved to sit in front of the mirror, several feet away from him.

"What was that about?" he said. "Why'd you move away so fast?"

I dodged the question, flushed and processing. "Nothing, just that was good, I guess."

He continued with this line of questioning over the next few days. I would be sitting in the common room at the studio and my phone would ding. I'd read, *So. Why'd you move away so fast? What were you feeling huh?*

I never knew exactly how to answer, so I continued to dodge: *Nothing.* ☺

Our conversations over the next few days never ventured far from the subject. As I sat in the passenger seat of his black Audi, staring out the window and counting the three exits on the 101 between the studio and his place, he would ask me for insights on his songs, waiting until I began speaking to ignore my answer, look over at me, and raise his eyebrows as if to say, *Sooooo, what'd you feel the other day?*

Avoiding the question became a sort of running gag. He'd ask; I'd dodge. He'd ask; I'd dodge.

One afternoon, after our usual few laps around his neighbourhood park, we walked into his building through the parking garage. He said, "Let's take a nap, then we'll go to the studio."

We went up the stairs, past the laundry room, and through the tropical outdoor lobby, potted plants lining the path and palm trees peeking over the terracotta rooftops. We walked into his place, closing the door behind us, leaving all the light on the other side. He slipped into the bathroom and said, "Lie down in my bed. It's comfier." I turned into his room and lay down on my side.

He came into the room, turned off the lights, and lay down beside me. He reached over and began running his hand down my leg, then back up to lay flat on my imperfect tummy, the tips of his fingers just barely under the top of my pants. He pushed himself up onto his elbow, licked his lips, and kissed me, pulling away a few moments later to say, "I knew you'd taste good."

We kissed for a few minutes, his fingers moving steadily down the front of my pants as my mind raced, trying to figure out what I was feeling. He moved my hand to feel him hard against my palm, then leaned in to kiss me again, his lips on my ears and moving down my neck toward my chest.

His mouth was wet and warm and moved with expert confidence. His body was tanned and tight, but I still couldn't figure out what I was feeling.

He kissed me again, then got up to go to the bathroom, leaving me to stare at the stucco ceiling in the dark, carpeted bedroom. I sat up on the side of the bed, watching him piss, his black tank crumpled above the top of his pants, revealing his sculpted abs and sun-kissed hip.

He fucked me for the first time a few days later, on the floor beside his bed, lit by the cold fluorescent light leaking through his open bathroom door.

The technical side of it felt good, being in the hands of someone whose hands had been on so many other someones. But something stood between me and my pleasure, a dark silhouette of my older, wiser future self, standing over us, whispering, "Is this really what you want, Hayley?"

tal

the job

Let's talk for a second about what being an L.A.-based songwriter looks like. When you start out, you are basically a professional blind-date speed dater. You sign to a publisher and then they start filling your calendar with the names and addresses of men. Men who are producers. For years I never saw another woman. Like, where are they keeping all the women?

In my experience as a freshly signed writer, there is no real thought put into these "dates." It's like, "Well, she's new to the city and we don't know who she's gonna fall in love with, so we'll say yes to everyone." Like Tinder with a pimp. Like your pimp runs your Tinder. He sits in a spacious office overlooking Beverly Hills, wearing a bright-orange leather jacket and a tilted green fedora adorned by a single black hawk feather, which he sometimes uses to dislodge bits of food from between his teeth. And he puts zero effort into considering compatibility. He's like, "Let's toss her around. Some combination will do something that will make somebody some money."

There's also an illusion of productivity that comes with being busy. In L.A., it is easy to be busy. It is easy to write a new song with a new person every single day. You can speedily collect songs, which you just as speedily dump into your "Never to Be Released by Any Artist Ever" folder. You get thrown into a pit of producers to test how prolific you can be. You get thrown into a pit of producers to learn how to operate in a studio, how to collaborate, how to be vulnerable, how to write. You get thrown into a pit of producers to see if you'll snap and move back to Winnipeg and open up a seat at the table for some girl from Alberta named Beth whose major ambition is to be signed even though she has no idea what signing to anyone means at all.

For my deal, Tal and his partner did a sort of joint venture with a major label. These arrangements seem like they would be a good idea. You have the power of a major label but the home-grown intimacy and focus of a small boutique production team. The issue is that each party passes the buck to the other. The label is like, "The production team will get her work," and the production team is like, "The label will get her work."

After I'd signed to Tal, any given day looked something like this:

- Wake up at Tal's. Usually in his bed.
- Eat Trader Joe's sausages, plantain chips, mango slices, and whatever carob-covered treat Tal decided was good for us.

- Listen to Tal do some sort of industry/sex/love-related monologue while doing one to three laps around the nearby park.
- Go to the studio.
- Sit alone in the lounge for three to five hours, hoping to be pulled into whatever session Tal has going on in his room.
- Check schedule and find the name and location of some adult male who also happens to be a producer.
- Borrow Tal's car and drive to stranger's house in the hills.
- Lose all phone reception.
- Inch open side gate and walk toward the setting sun to the muted sounds of drums or keyboards or guitars.
- Hope I'm in the right place.
- Knock.
- Sit in a small room with a stranger and write and record a song for four to six hours.
- Get an email of the finished song (if I'm lucky), then go home and never see the producer again.

What I didn't realize for the first several years I lived in L.A. is that I was supposed to be finding my musical husbands. I was supposed to be "dating" with the intention of creating a kind of polygamous community for myself. I was supposed to be finding specific partners for specific jobs. Like, go to John if you want a nice romantic date night; call up Alvin if you want to go skydiving or snorkelling; email Bruno if you don't want to walk right the next day.

Nobody really teaches you what this industry looks like or how to be signed well.

I thought the finish line was getting signed. Like, once I put my name on a piece of paper, everything would fall into place. I would confidently run my pen along the pages of a twenty-page contract, excitedly stacking bright yellow *Sign here* and *Initial here* tabs along the edge of the table and suddenly have a career.

This is not at all how it went down for me. I floated in and out of studios with no real intention or strategy. I sat in Tal's studio while he lectured me on how I needed to have intention and strategy without offering any sort of breadcrumbs or constructive information on what those things really were.

Tal's mentoring strategy was like a teacher saying "Know how to read" to a class of six-year-olds.

earl

gold joint in a white mercedes

Nearly a year after I met and was aggressively hit on by a certain producer, my phone dinged and there he was again.

Can I take you for dinner? he texted.

Aren't you married? I replied.

No. I'd like to explain over dinner.

I agreed.

Earl invited me for dinner at a dim, iconic Melrose institution where one of his friends was a bartender. I was still at a point with Tal where I was trying to convince myself that it wasn't going to develop into anything at all. Where I was attempting to flex some freedom and gain some distance with tall, dark, handsome distractions.

I came right from a session. A session as in me in a windowless room with a producer writing a song to hurl in Rihanna's direction, hoping that my feelings would resonate with her feelings and she'd cut the song and release it as a huge single and enable me to immediately purchase my dream home, or at least groceries.

I lingered outside the restaurant wearing an outfit that said, *I am not trying to impress you* — ripped jeans, black Ramones T-shirt, green army jacket, and filthy white sneakers. Sitting on a bench, I watched Earl pull up to the valet in a white Mercedes and considered my emasculated Honda parked two blocks away at an expired meter.

Earl walked around his car. He was dressed in black from head to toe, like one giant walking leather glove. I shoved my hands into my jacket pockets, quietly regretting my outfit choice.

He suggestively kissed my cheek. Then he placed his hand on my lower back, gestured toward the door, and said, "Let me feed you." He led me into the restaurant with the confidence of someone who had done this a lot, nodding at the staff in a way that made me think he had maybe been there the previous evening with another girl.

He guided me toward a quiet corner booth, never losing contact between his hand and the small of my back. We nuzzled into either side. I clocked his eyes noticing my briefly exposed clavicle as I tugged my jacket off. He smiled the way you smile when you not-so-accidentally find your brother's porn in his underwear drawer: the smile of a devious discovery with devious plans.

An older male career waiter came over. We ordered dirty martinis, calamari, and a bloody steak.

We spent the first hour catching up the way you do when you haven't seen someone in a year, running over the wheres, the whats, the whens, the hows. Then, with the assistance of a third martini, we launched into the whos.

He told me about the sixteen years he'd spent with his high-school sweetheart. They'd gotten married shortly after I met him, then almost immediately separated.

He gestured to the waiter, who then appeared with the best apple pie I have ever had in my life — basically just a bowl of scalding hot butter with caramelized apples, flaky pastry, and speckled vanilla ice cream.

Earl leaned over the table and said, "It's kinda douchey, but I have a joint rolled in twenty-four-karat gold papers. I say we leave and walk and smoke it."

The drinks had made me tipsy, the dessert had made me drunk, so I said yes.

I'll often reach for my wallet as a courtesy, but when a man has rekindled a year-long crush with a swanky dinner invite and has a gold joint in his pocket, I let him pay.

We wandered up and down Melrose, smoking a gold joint like we were in a rap video. We passed his white Mercedes and I thought, *This gold joint was in that white Mercedes.* Dancing in and out of life-shaking epiphanies and sensations, we floated up and off the pavement in a cloud of gold smoke.

After a couple hours of walking, when I was at a slightly more responsible stage in my drunkenness, he led me to my car. He opened the driver's-side door for me, his back in the Melrose traffic. I nudged in to sit behind my steering wheel.

Standing with the door propped open, one hand on the hood, he leaned in and kissed me. Then, my arms at my sides, my chin up, he pushed the top of my head into the headrest and slipped his hand down my pants and began fingering me, his ass in Melrose traffic at 10:00 p.m. on a Thursday. Pulling his lips away from mine, he watched me take it for a few minutes, then took his hand out, put his fingers in his mouth, and closed the door.

The evening was followed by my receiving a number of his elegant, faceless, homemade phone pornos. Then a couple weeks later, after he'd cancelled plans half a dozen times, he messaged me. He said he was looking for a real relationship and felt I only wanted him for sex.

famous, nameless songwriter

don't ask

As we sat on a Toronto streetcar, inching along Queen Street in the thick of rush hour, my friend Jane turned to me and said, "Oh my god, I forgot to tell you. We got a session with him. He's down to write with us." I was twenty, fresh to Toronto, and had just started songwriting with any shred of ambition. My goal as a songwriter was very small for a very long time. Small and singular: reveal feelings to _____ [insert man's name here].

This session was not going to turn into another love letter to my teenage crush. This was a real opportunity. This was a big, famous songwriter willing to write with two brand-new, no-name, no-reputation writers he'd never met before.

Three days later, we were walking in a residential neighbourhood, passing rows of homes so specific to Toronto, mammoth and deep-set and nearly pressed against each other. Jane motioned to her left and said, "Here we are." She reached for the doorknob as she continued. "Also, he said we might have to help him with something before we write. It's like some game that he and his childhood friend play sometimes? I didn't get exactly what he was saying, but we're supposed to let ourselves in."

We did as we were instructed and pushed open the door. "Hello," we said in unison, giggling uncomfortably like two little girls accidentally left alone in a department store overnight, a perfect balance of confusion and nervousness and excitement in our voices.

We moved fearfully down a long, dark hallway, passing a shelf of awards and a wall of photos of musical icons. At the end of the hall, we noticed a light on in the kitchen and we heard muffled sounds of someone in distress. We stepped around the corner and found our famous co-writer in his underwear, his legs and arms tied to a chair, and his mouth stuffed with a bright-red gag.

When he saw us, he cried his muffled cry a bit louder, the way 100 percent of girls getting rescued in movies do. Adrenalin peaking in a surge of hope and panic at the prospect of being rescued or, even worse, the possibility of being so close to freedom and somehow fucking it up.

Without questioning what was going on, Jane walked around the back of the chair to start unravelling the fraying rope that bound his hands together. I pulled the red gag out of his mouth and freed his feet from the wooden chair legs. He gasped for air like a kid in a pageant, over the top and perhaps with the hope of winning some sort of ribbon.

We pulled the remaining rope from around his waist and he stood up. "I'm gonna grab some water," he said, then disappeared up the stairs, dragging the rope still hooked around one ankle.

Jane and I sat on the couch outside of the kitchen, looking at each other like, *Wait, what?* Our bodies spasmed with silent laughter.

I had started plucking Jane's guitar by the time he came back twenty minutes later, fully clothed. As if nothing had happened he said, "Oh, that's nice. Let's write to that!"

We tossed out lyrics and shaped verses and sculpted the chorus until, a couple hours later, we deemed it done. He led us back down the dark hallway to the door and said, "That was fun. Let's do it again sometime."

dad

delusions of grandeur

I have this recurring dream that isn't really a dream at all — it's a memory that plays on a loop in my head, tangled up with scenes from Disney movies, a few loitering phone numbers, and bits of commercial jingles from twenty years ago.

I'm at an indoor public pool in Winnipeg. It's the early '90s and I'm six. The pool area seems endless to me, as a three-foot-something kid. My hair smells like chlorine, and cool water drips down the braid pressed to my bright-pink polka-dot bathing suit.

I'm at the end of the line for the diving board. Nine kids, mimicking maturity, bravely inch forward, their arms wrapped around their tiny vibrating bodies, trying to conceal the weakness of being cold. One at a time, the children reach the plank. Any insincere bravado melts like a cheap birthday candle and the jumper becomes only six again. Whatever else they are, they are six. They are scared and six. Or nervous and six. Or reckless and six.

Every sound in the room manages to be the same volume. The echo of a splash booms as loudly as a parent screaming or a nanny attempting to whisper a secret: "So yeah, Ally, we all just heard you've been having an affair with the mother of the two kids you take care of."

It's almost my turn. My way-too-big-for-my-age feet are pruney and indented with the pattern of the metal diving board. A boy is taking forever to jump. He's been clutching on to the board, and I am quietly enjoying his total lack of grace. I am casually leaning on the railing, picking at my nails, waiting for my turn.

The boy's parents are excitedly cheering him on from the other end of the pool. "Come on, Jason! You got this!" Eventually, he smiles and leans forward into a spectacular bellyflop. His panicking parents fish his flimsy, sobbing body out of the pool, and now it's my turn.

If I had been chewing gum, I definitely would have stuck it behind my ear. If I had been smoking a cigarette, I definitely would have taken one final badass puff and flicked it into the kiddie pool.

I walk toward the edge of the diving board, then pause and slowly turn around to look at the line of kids waiting to jump in after me.

I open my mouth and say, "Hey, what does your dad do?"

The kid up next says, "My daddy wears a suit and goes to the bank."

I smile. I smile like the Joker. I smile like a fucking asshole and say, "Oh, yeah? Well my dad is Fred Penner."

He required no job description. No title. He got to be only his name.

I flip my perfectly dishevelled fish braid over my shoulder, do a perfect little swan dive, and swim to the edge of the pool. I pull myself out of the bright-blue water as if in slow motion. I feel the envious eyes of the remaining plank divers burning a hole in the back of my head as I walk into the towel my dad is holding open, his arms extended as if to say, *How much do I love you? Thiiiiis much.* He picks me up and I turn my face into his shoulder, finally able to reveal my chattering teeth to only him. I can be weak and real with only him. And I am warm and dry and safe pressed against his chest in the yoke-yellow terry cloth.

dad

shadows

The thing about having a famous parent is that you are never alone. Not really. I walk into every room with him invisibly behind me, like a transparent bodyguard. His name hovers over me, offering any new person in my life the promise of something special. The pressure is entirely lifted off my shoulders. My specialness gets to live in my name alone, where I couldn't remove it if I tried. There's nothing I can say to drop or misplace it. It comes with me. For those of you who aren't Canadian, he's basically Mr. Rogers. Like TV-show-for-twelve-years, sparkle-in-your-eyes-when-you-think-of-him Mr. Rogers. And it's real. There is no behind the curtain. He is who he appears to be — and isn't that nice in a world of mirages?

When I was growing up, one of my favourite things to do was to go grocery shopping with my dad. At twelve, thirteen, fourteen, I'd sneakily slide my hand onto the shelves and slip a couple pregnancy tests or boxes of condoms into the cart, tucking them under the blueberries and cereal, forcing him to notice the contraband in front of some poor checkout person who had to handle his fame and embarrassment all at once.

As we strolled through the aisles, I would watch the faces of the men and women and children around us, who were trying to hide their excitement. They would whisper and point to each other. Parents would kneel beside their children and motion, grinning, at our impenetrable little bubble, rolling down the aisles on a Safeway shopping cart as if it were a float in the Macy's Thanksgiving Day Parade.

My dad often didn't notice. He would be deep in his shopping list while I smiled politely on his behalf at the vibrating audience around us. I would nod my head and gingerly wave like the Queen, giving them a silent *Yes, it is him, and no, I don't even have to try to get him to love me.*

Then there were the people who just had to come up and say hello. These run-ins took a variety of shapes. There was the girl who almost pulled her hair out, dropping her ice cream cone on the ground and screaming at us, literally clutching her chest, hyperventilating like he was a Beatle: "You're … oh my god … oh my god. It's you … oh my god." There were the respectful drive-by sightings, just a voice passing with an outstretched hand in a restaurant or café: "Hey, Fred, just wanted to say how much we appreciate your work." Then there were the six-degrees-of-Kevin-Bacon sightings: "Sorry to bother you, but my friend Joseph's sister's best friend just started working with this guy named Martin who was in cadets with you forty years ago." These were the most impressive because inevitably, every time, my dad would respond with something like, "Oh wow, Martin McGilvery! Tell him and Mary that I say hello!"

The thing about being the type of famous that comes with being a children's entertainer is that every run-in is full of love and nostalgia and joy. Every fan grew up with him in their living room or den or bedroom each morning for twelve years. As his daughter, it was impossible to not feel a bit special, having come from the source of so much joy. And it is impossible to not feel like that magic must be rubbing off on me in some way. Like I'm special by proximity.

The other thing about growing up with a famous parent is that you develop a very intimate relationship with shadows — the cool, shaded, protective shadows of branches and buildings and men. There have been chapters in my life when I hated his shadow, when all I wanted was to see an unshaded sky above me. I wanted unspectacular shoes to step into, unextraordinary heritage to inherit. Then there was the rest of the time. The rest of the time, which was most of the time. That most of the time shielded me from rain and snow and sleet and pain, and above all else, it shielded me from feeling ordinary, my biggest fear of all.

So, yes, it is unsurprising that I dive in headfirst with any man I deem extraordinary, particularly when that specialness is talent based. Talent is kryptonite for me. If you're talented, meet me, Hayley, your brand-new, albeit slightly busted-up punching bag. You don't have to call me back or offer me any sort of improved quality of life. You can sit back and expect to be showered in entirely unearned gifts and love and consideration. Oh, also, you totally don't have to be faithful to me. Just give me a few days and casually say you're sorry once, maybe toss in a *you look pretty today*, and I will lovingly nuzzle back into a fetal position at your feet. Because if you're special, I must be special, too.

The value from my father that I held on to and carried into my first relationships was not his incredible kindness or generosity or care or consideration. It was his fame and his talent, dangerous things to value in all places, but particularly in Los Angeles.

tal

six men and a lady

The options were (a) one of the bare mattresses in the hall or (b) one of the couches in the living room. I went with secret option (c) wedging a toddler's mattress into the water-heater closet off the kitchen. The thought of not having a door to sleep behind in a house with six men did not sit well with me. I bought a foot-stool from Goodwill, shoved it beside the mattress, and called it a bedside table. I stole flowers from our neighbours' yards and put them in a glass of tap water, which I placed on the stool like a proper grown-up lady.

Tal paid for this place to house producers and songwriters, as well as the three musicians who had moved to L.A. to start a band with him. I had been living in Tal's second bedroom for a few weeks when he decided to move me into his new artist/producer storage facility.

The house sat cradled between a giant Macy's parking lot and the entrance to the 101 freeway. The living room, at the front of the house, featured two long, shapeless, brown blob couches, on which slept one of Tal's producers. Past the living room, on the right, you would find one of the house's two bathrooms. The other was just outside the kitchen, across from a double mattress on wheels that slept another artist Tal's company was courting. The bathrooms were white and speckled with anywhere from one to a thousand hairs shed by any number of men. I got a membership at 24 Hour Fitness exclusively for the showers. The four proper bedrooms were occupied by Tal's bandmates and his brother/my manager, Tobias.

Every morning, we would take the twenty-minute walk under the freeway to the studio as a group, these six men and me. We would arrive and they would play basketball with their shirts off and I would watch from the roof behind the net. Then they would go into studios to work and I would wait. I would pretend to be productive on my computer in the common room and wait for them to be done so we could go see a movie as a group, then get dropped off back at our frat house.

I lived in the house for only a couple months before Tal moved me back into his apartment. And I mostly loved it. It was so disgusting and messy and full of testicles, but it was kind of perfect. Like, Canadian girl moves to L.A. and lives in a closet like a wizard. I would pull my knees into my chest and delight in the filth of it, fantasizing about my future E! True Hollywood Story: "In the next hour, we will investigate the order of events that led this confident young Canadian woman to end up living in a closet next to a water heater in a house with six men. This is the story of Hayley Gene Penner, the *E! True Hollywood Story*."

Tal temporarily moved me out of his two-bedroom apartment and into the house after we'd started sleeping together. During the time I lived in the giant man cave, he also got back together with both his out-of-town girlfriend, Molly, and his local girlfriend, June, though I didn't know that until much later. Then he moved me back into his apartment, I guess once he felt both those relationships were stable and secure. I rolled up my little mattress and left my bedside table in the kitchen to pursue its true destiny as an actual footstool.

river

keep your friends close and the
corkscrew in your pocket closer

From the back patio of a tiny dive bar in Hollywood, I spotted him dipping in and out of view, appearing and disappearing between expressive arms, boozy conversations, and flirtatious looks. He passed my breakable six-foot-something rule, and his piercing blue eyes and scraggly black beard beckoned me from the middle of a group of only slightly less hot man friends. Totally trashed, he passed me a bar napkin with his number on it and screamed directly into my ear. "I'm River. I have a place

in the hills. Come over tomorrow night and I'll make you dinner. You like fish?"

I woke up the next morning on my bare mattress in Tal's
second bedroom. I rolled over to find the bar napkin with the
messy black writing of River with the piercing blue eyes. June
was fast asleep in Tal's bed, and we had begun the nauseating
process of lying to her together. On the nights she came by, I
would sleep in the spare bedroom, in front of the wall of mirrors. We would hug and maybe have dinner all together, then I
would slip into my room to hate myself for the night. I would
stare at the shared wall and listen to her giggle and to him sort
of growl, the way he did.

In moments like those, impulsively going out with a stranger
felt like asserting some control over my life. Like, "Look, Tal. I'm
unaffected. I'm dating."

As I was getting dressed, putting on a blue summer dress,
River sent me his address. I filled my purse with the ingredients to
make a fresh chocolate cake after dinner and then popped a wine
opener in my pocket. This is one of those seemingly unremarkable
actions that, when examined, reveals a world of repressed feelings
only recognizable in the retelling. My hand, like an animal's tail,
with feelings and thoughts and motivations of its own, put the
wine opener in my pocket as a potential weapon, just in case.

I pulled up to a beautiful home on a winding road in the
Laurel Canyon hills. Unable to find parking, I texted him to open
the gate and let me into the driveway.

I realized, the second it closed behind me, that he now had
full control of when I could leave.

He ran around the corner of the house as I hopped out of
my car. I looked back, registering the locking of the gate behind
my back bumper. He was even more stunning than I remembered,
with a giant smile and those piercing blue eyes. He wrapped his
forearms against my lower back and pulled me tightly against him.

He led me into his house. We chatted casually as I walked into the kitchen so I could put down my cake fixin's. As I pulled my heavy bag off my shoulder and plopped it on the counter, I felt him walk up behind me.

He bent his knees, reached down, and began running his hands up my legs, under my dress, and around my inner thighs. My heart pounding like a skipping T. Rex, I turned around to face him and was met with his plunging tongue and swelling chest arching me back over the counter as he ran his hands up my dress and around my neck. He pushed his fingers into my cheeks, encouraging my mouth to open, and he kissed me.

I kissed him back, laughed uncomfortably, then playfully pushed him off.

I excused myself and went to the bathroom. Standing in front of the elegant mirror, which was lined by three perfect rows of monochromatic grooming ointments, I reached into my pocket, grazing my hand against the corkscrew, and grabbed my iPhone. I quickly texted a friend: *Sorry this is weird. I'm at 555 Kirkwood Drive off of Laurel Canyon. If I don't text you every hour or so, just come here.*

I quieted the warning lump in the pit of my stomach and opened the bathroom door to find him directly outside. "Let me give you a tour!" he said excitedly.

He started guiding me around his home as if it were ours. Pointing to pieces of artwork on the walls like a curator in a gallery, saying, "Remember when we picked up this piece in Germany that one summer?" and "Remember how you thought this one was too expensive, but I convinced you to get it after reminding you how hard you work, how much you deserve to treat yourself?"

I laughed, hoping it was a joke I just didn't understand.

His tour ended back in the living room. I sat down on the couch, my hand in my pocket, clutching the corkscrew. Like, when do I make the call to thrust it into his throat? At what point is that justifiable? How scared do I have to be to run? At what point is that acceptable?

Unable to sit down, he manically paced around the room, telling me how he had been arrested a number of times, used to be a heroin addict, and tried to kill himself to get a girlfriend back. At some point during this monologue, he plopped a plate of fish and vegetables in front of me on the coffee table. I stared the dead fish in its one exposed bulbous dead fish eye as he told me how lucky I was to be chosen by him, how he could have picked anyone.

Eventually, he went to the bathroom, and I went to the kitchen to text my friend. Not wanting him to feel like it was the last time he was going to see me, I decided to play it very cool and make the cake. I started beating the eggs.

I pulled my bag closer to me on the counter as I felt him come up behind me again. He wrapped his arms around me, grabbed my left forearm with one hand, mimed giving me a shot of heroin with the other, then made a sound as if he were cumming.

"Wanna go for a walk?"

I have seen enough *SVU* to know that you die in the hills. You get clubbed in the back of the head, raped, and buried. So naturally I said, "Okay."

He started to lead me up into the hills in the darkness, still babbling nonsensically. We stood looking out over the shimmering city, his hand on my back, sliding down my spine.

As if I'd stepped into a walk-in cooler, my entire body froze at his touch. I said, "Wow, beautiful. I'm cold. Let's go back." I let gravity sprint me down the hill.

When we got back into the house, I grabbed my bag, feeling that I could safely leave, that he would conceivably believe he would see me again.

He started begging me to spend the night. After I said no a number of times, he tried a new approach. "Just come lie down with me for a minute."

I felt like the only way out was in, so I said, "Okay."

He led me back down the hallway, past the paintings we had "purchased on vacation together," toward the bedroom tucked in the back of the house. His breath heavier and his body thicker, he lay down on his king-sized bed and patted the green comforter, gesturing for me to join him. I lay stiffly beside him, resting my arms in an X over my chest like an open casket corpse.

Instantly, he pulled my favourite man-move: the Whip It Out.

I looked over at his giant, gorgeous cock and momentarily considered it. But feeling the corkscrew against my hip, I reminded myself that I had spent the previous three hours uncomfortable and scared. I said, "Listen, you don't get to touch me tonight, but you take care of yourself."

Staring me in the eye, he smiled and started. He throbbed in his hand, doing tiny, spasm-y microcrunches in response to his own touch. Moaning, he rolled onto his side to push it against my hip.

I recoiled and got off the bed, as touching was prohibited.

As I moved toward the door, he followed me. With his dick in one hand, he backed me against the closet door, lifted his other arm above my head to stabilize himself, then pump, pump, pumped and came on my feet.

Feeling him temporarily deflated, I thought it a good time to say good night.

He pulled up his pants and pecked my neck as if to say, *Thanks, tuts*, and then escorted me to my car. I got in, watched the gate open, and pulled out as quickly and calmly as I could, his beautiful body and piercing blue eyes lit up in my headlights.

I drove back to Tal's, parked beside June's car, and threw out my shoes.

kirsti

lookin' for love in all the wrong places

One time, I put peanut butter on my tit while babysitting at our neighbours' house in River Heights. I had put the kid to bed and thought I'd see if the dog might lick the peanut butter off. I was eleven. But then I was so terrified they might have a nanny cam that I stopped the procedure before I found out whether the dog would do it or not. I wiped the peanut butter off with the back of my hand and started crying out of shame and fear, alone in a living room just a few panes of glass away from my parents', one house over.

I had been quietly trying to get all my friends to make out with me for years. Male friends, female friends, older, younger, close family friends, cousins, whoever I could get my hands on, really. Starting with daycare, where I had to be put into a private napping zone because if they left me with all the other kids, they'd find me twiddling some kid's diddle five minutes into sleepy time. I was four.

Next, it was Frances. I was nine. I'd attempt to run my hands under her skirt between rows of crisp white dress shirts in her parents' basement laundry room. In my memory there were hundreds of them, like we were lost in a large dry-cleaning business, and it was somehow dusk indoors, and the room was misty and smelled like baby powder as we playfully hid behind endless lines of starchy linens.

Then it was Tabby. Trying to feel her up in a sauna when I was ten. We had made out a few times during sleepovers. I held back my disappointment when she told me she didn't want to do it anymore, on the dock at her cabin — again, at dusk.

Then came Kirsti.

I was a well-liked elementary school student. Undiscriminating, and friends with the nerds and the cool kids and the weird kids and the artsy kids. Like, if you had a neck brace or stammer or lazy eye, you could still sit with me.

So when Kirsti arrived to our class in grade six, our teacher pulled me aside and said, "Hayley, I'd love for you to show Kirsti around. Be her friend? Make her feel welcome?"

Kirsti was sweet and funny and weird in the way I prefer all my friends to be. Her dad worked for a company that organized hot-air-balloon trips, so one summer we ballooned above the city as my dad drove beneath us, taking photos of our plump silhouette in the prairie sky.

By some miraculous twist of fate, she was like me.

Her mom's place was conveniently located a couple blocks from ours. My mother was not the "Get on your bike and go discover the world" type; my siblings and I were driven to our destinations.

It started in the purely unsophisticated manner in which most sexual encounters begin, a shared bed and two sets of legs testing each other's responsiveness, testing the recoil or the lean in, measuring the subtle willingness based on the seconds spent pressed together.

I rolled to face the middle of the bed. She rolled to face the middle of the bed, lifting and releasing the creased indentation dividing us, and settling us together under one blanket. We kissed and touched and looked.

Our sleepovers evolved over the school year. Taking turns being the giver or the receiver, the doctor, the patient.

We took our little show all over Winnipeg: my parents' place, her mom's, and eventually her dad's. She spent the least amount of time at her dad's, which was good because he lived farther away, so organizing sleepovers at his place was tricky.

Our whole arrangement died at her dad's. He nearly caught us one night. I was running my hand down the front of her cotton drawstring pyjama bottoms when he knocked on the door and entered the room simultaneously, the way parents do. The knock is a notification, not a question.

She aggressively recoiled from my touch as the door opened. The hall light poured in with him, then sucked out behind him.

I reached to run my hand along her thigh once he was gone. She shifted away and said, "I don't want to do this anymore."

marlo

trying stuff

My adolescent dabbling with the lady folk resurfaced only once, casually, many years later. That is, of course, if you don't count the fact that I watch lesbian porn exclusively.

Her hand brushed against mine as she poured a bag of chips into a metal bowl on the large wooden dining table in my parents' empty house.

I almost always took advantage of my empty family home when my parents were away by having any number of friends over. It was less about trashing the place, or even about friendship, and more that I felt like having people around lessened my chances of getting murdered by a wandering burglar/serial killer. Or I imagined the burglar would only kill the first person he saw upon breaking in, maybe the first few. Since I slept on the third floor, his murderous rage would be satiated before he got to me. At the very least, I would be able to shimmy down the drainpipe to the gasping sounds of my poor friends being butchered on the floor beneath me.

I was nineteen and just a few days away from moving to Toronto. I had invited over two close girlfriends that night, Marlo and Cheliza. We sat around the table, drinking and talking and eating and laughing. We cackled the way old friends do, drinking wine from my parents' huge, hilarious pottery chalices and running backward in time, remembering junior-high-school teachers' names and crying in hallways and lingering crushes and hiding in locker rooms during slow songs at high-school dances.

Wine spewed out of Marlo's nose as I reminded her of the time I almost got expelled for blasphemy in my private Mennonite school. I had turned Jesus into a woman and named her Jesusy.

Somewhere between the chips and the wine, we got into my relationship with Kirsti in grade six. I described our scandalous year-long affair as I collected the bowls and napkins and bits of sticky socializing debris. Marlo smiled like a kid who'd managed to get into a final exam with a trail of blotchy, scribbled answers written in defiant blue ink up her left forearm. The smile of someone who knew exactly what to do.

I wedged the wooden pole into the sliding glass doors in an additional attempt to keep the murderers out for one more night, then began locking up the house. Cheliza grabbed her stuff and headed to the front door as Marlo said, "Do you mind if I just crash here? I'm wiped."

This was obviously good news for me because, again, murderers.

I turned on the alarm and tossed the last of the trash into the sink. We walked upstairs.

"Pick a room, any room. I'm staying in there," I said, motioning to my parents' room. My third-floor suite was in total disarray in preparation for my move. My mattress was leaning against a wall, while the rest of the room featured small heaps of clothes I needed to sift through, heaps like cotton islands in a sea of pink carpet.

I grabbed my toiletry bag off the hallway shelf and went into the bathroom to get ready for bed. I washed and brushed and came back into the now-dark hallway. Hearing the shuffling of sheets, I opened the door to my parents' room to find a fully naked Marlo tucking herself into bed.

"This okay?" she said.

I was incredibly uncomfortable. I'd known her since we were kids and this felt odd and incestuous. So I said, "Oh, um, sure?"

I perched half my butt on the edge of the bed and slipped my legs in under the blankets, nearly falling off the side. "Good night," I said, and I leaned over to flick off the bedside lamp.

I felt her shift beside me, the sort of deliberate movements of someone who is trying to let you know they are not asleep and have no real intention of falling asleep. I have now employed this particular technique with many men. Like, maybe if I exhale heavily and unnaturally and adjust my position several times in a row, he will shake awake and suddenly match my Olympic-level sex drive.

She shifted over and laid her hand on my imperfect tummy, waiting for me to answer the question she was asking with her touch. I said, "I'm not gonna do anything to you but, like, you can try to do, like … stuff … to … me … if you want."

This felt like the closest thing to a no that I could muster up.

She slipped her hand down the front of my pants as I squeezed my eyes shut in the darkness, quietly willing it to stop.

It is hard to say no to someone you love. It is hard to reject somebody you care about. It is hard to not want to protect a person's feelings when you know you have the power to.

I counted down in my head from thirty, thinking, *Once I get to zero I can respectfully ask her to stop. Like, thirty seconds is a totally reasonable length to see if something moves me.*

Three, two, one. "Yeah, I think maybe, stop? I'm gonna go sleep upstairs."

She immediately pulled her hand away and said, "Of course."

I grabbed my pillow and held it to my chest as I walked up the carpeted steps to the third floor. I crashed on the giant green beanbag pillow under the window, and we never talked about it again.

jude

wrap it up

Jude was my only reciprocated high-school crush. I liked him not only because he was cute and funny and weird and had this chubby bottom lip I found myself thinking about during science and math and gym. He was also popular and a perfect distraction from my persistent loving feelings for my best friend, Paul.

We'll get to Paul.

Jude was my love interest in our school's rendition of *The Sound of Music*. He was the Rolfe to my Liesl.

Our first kissing rehearsal was marked on the cafeteria door, just a week away. Bold print beside the scheduled scene said, "'I Am 16' — Full song — No more marking."We both knew what that meant.

He caught up with me after a rehearsal as I walked to the parking lot. I quietly thanked God for making my dad ten minutes late so Jude had the opportunity to scoot up behind me and ask if he could take me somewhere on Saturday night. I think he didn't want our first kiss to be fake.

I spent most of Saturday trying to figure out what to wear, trying desperately to disguise my adult-woman body, to transform it into the shapeless teenage frame I'd always wanted.

Jude walked up to our front door and knocked with the sole purpose of impressing my father, who in some incestuous way was his father, too. My dad was a sort of surrogate parent for my entire generation, parenting them from their TV screens every morning for twelve years, and in the process planting only the slightest of messiah complexes in me, the daughter of.

I zipped up my not-nearly-warm-enough winter jacket and quickly, passively, waved goodbye to my parents over my shoulder.

We drove out of my neighbourhood, over the bridge by our high school, and around the corner into Wolseley. Jude turned down a quiet dead-end street and parked in front of a large, abandoned-looking house. He reached into the back seat, grabbed a small black duffel bag, which he slung over his shoulder, and said, "Here we are."

By sixteen, I already had a flawlessly formed fear of everything, courtesy of my mother, so as I followed him into the house, I hummed the theme song to *The Simpsons* in the hopes that it would drown out the tiny voice whispering, *You're about to die.*

He pulled a key out of his pocket and opened the front door. With his hand on the small of my back, he guided me into the totally empty house. The front door opened into a huge living room, a king-sized Moroccan carpet, the only sign of life in the otherwise empty space, the couchless, tableless, electricity-less space.

He pulled a candle out of the black duffel bag, lit it, and began to give me a tour of the house, explaining that this was his family's old home. It was on the market but hadn't sold yet. He led me up the first set of stairs. I clutched the back of his shirt, half expecting some long-limbed slippery thing to reach out from one of the dozens of dark corners and pull me into what I know now as the Upside Down.

He motioned to one more set of stairs. A somehow wet, rickety, creaking set of stairs leading up to the attic. The tiny voice ran its sharp nails down the nape of my neck, whispering, *You're gonna die.*

Up those stairs we found the only piece of furniture in the entire house, a single mattress on a metal bed frame in the middle of a pitch-black room. Rejecting any consideration of bed activities, my body turned me around as I blurted out, "Cool house." Then I walked back down to the second floor.

Jude followed me down. "Let's go in here," he said, motioning toward what I assumed was his bedroom at the front of the house. He opened his black duffel bag and pulled out a blanket, a few more candles, a bag of chips, a tub of dip, and a small bottle of wine. I smiled, allowing myself to recognize, at least for a moment, that this was all meant to be sweet and romantic and it was perhaps *SVU*'s fault that I couldn't see it like that.

My moment of seeing the romance in it all came to a screeching halt. We were sitting on the blanket in the candlelight, laughing, talking, eating, when I heard something downstairs. In reality, it was just the sound of an old house. It was just an old house stretching or breathing or yawning or creaking, because that's what old houses do.

But in my head it was a large serial killer whose particular tastes were exclusively teenage girls with adult-woman bodies.

I blew out three of the four candles, leapt up, and said, "Cool room. Let's go back downstairs." I figured I'd be able to more easily escape the clutches of the serial killer if I was on a floor with a number of exits.

I stood by the door as Jude collected the chips, dip, blanket, and remaining lit candle. He shoved all but the candle into his small black duffel bag, probably feeling a bit defeated, then led us down the stairs by the dim, flickering, terrifying light of one single flame.

We walked into the giant living room, both of us laughing at me together.

He said, "Have you ever been rolled up in a carpet?"

I furrowed my brow, not because I was searching for misplaced memories of being rolled up in a carpet, but out of pure surprise at the question itself.

"No, I have not been rolled up in a carpet." *Do I ask him if he has?*

"You want to be?" he said.

I thought, *Weird*. I said, "Okay."

He put down the black duffel. "'K, lie down along this side of the carpet with your arms at your sides, and keep your head out the top so you can breathe."

Giggling nervously, I lay down.

He bent over and rolled me toward the window, the dark room spinning as he cocooned me in four, five, six rolls of carpet. The final roll left me facing the ceiling, my head and neck poking out of the top like a hot dog poking out of a hot dog bun.

He straddled the carpet for a second, a foot on either side of my paralyzed body. Looking down at me, half-lit by the yellow light of the street lanterns leaking into the room, he said, "Are you ready?"

I suddenly envisioned him pulling out a chainsaw or axe or machete to sloppily remove my head from the rest of my body.

He stepped to one side and grabbed the exposed edge of the carpet. Squatting down, he looked at me with his dark eyes, his skin lily white. He licked his delicious fat lips and whispered, "One, two, three," then stood up, unravelling the rug in one swift motion and hurling my body to the other side of the room.

The room eventually stopped spinning as I lay on my back. I turned my head to see him keeled over, laughing at me, backlit by the giant window at the front of the house. I propped myself up on my elbows and started laughing, too — a reaction, I imagine, he was relieved to see.

We kissed the following Thursday, at 4:00 p.m., in the fluorescent-lit cafeteria, with the hovering stench of burnt vegetable oil in the air and our music teacher's booming, operatic voice howling stage directions in our ears.

dad

forty below

Winnipeg winter makes you feel alive by reminding you how close you are to death. How easy it would be to just pick a spot, sit down, and die.

This cold would wrap around our homes just in time for my birthday on November 5. Then, inevitably, every year when even we thought it couldn't possibly get colder, it would — on New Year's Eve.

I was fifteen. I sat cross-legged on the floor of my bedroom, in whatever outfit I thought gave me the best chance of getting my best friend, Paul, to finally realize he was in love with me. Most likely some colourful corduroy pants with a belt so I could work my new belly-button piercing — the piercing I got solely because I had overheard him saying his ex had one — into the conversation. Like, "Man, this belt buckle is really rubbing up against my new piercing." Like, "Image planted. Go ahead and start falling in love with me, Paul."

I reached behind me and pulled one of my journals out from under the pillow. I tore a movie-ticket-sized piece from a page and grabbed the pen that had rolled under my bed. I began writing what I most wanted in life, my deepest desires, in all caps as tiny as possible.

I wrote in all caps as tiny as possible because that's how Paul wrote. He had this very specific way of writing, in unreasonably tiny all caps. So I wrote out my wish list as if it were in his handwriting, which somehow made me feel closer to him.

I rolled up my tiny wish list, kissed it with my eyes closed, and tucked it into my front pocket.

"Out the door in five," my dad yelled from the kitchen.

I sat in the front passenger seat of our family minivan, my legs freezing from the six-second walk from the house to the garage. My dad flipped through the radio stations as he drove me to Paul's house party. He did his slow-motion car dance, punching toward the windshield to the Dire Straits song "Money for Nothing" as we pulled onto the Disraeli Bridge.

"Can you pull over? I wrote this little list and I want to hurl it off the bridge."

He smiled, flicked on his blinker, and pulled into the far-right lane.

I wedged my hand under a few thick layers and pulled the tiny scroll out of my pocket. Once again, I held it to my lips with my eyes pressed shut.

As we approached the highest point of the bridge, my dad rolled down my window. The deadly cold rushed in, filling the entire van in a split second.

I took one deep, intentional breath and extended my arm into the rushing frozen air. I watched the white corners of my tiny wish list begin to peek through my fingers. Then, against the will of the wind, I opened my hand and released my capsule of dreams into the frigid Winnipeg night.

The party was fun. Paul did not realize he was deeply in love with me, but it was fun. I did some underage drinking and ate dip and made some jokes some people laughed at and yelled "Happy New Year!" at midnight.

I moved to Toronto when I was nineteen. Four years after that New Year's Eve.

My final birthday as a Winnipeg local was, in many ways, no different from the eighteen that preceded it. The cold settled in just before Halloween, starting with that solemn blue sky the night before the first big snow.

I got some money in personalized envelopes, offerings of protection from my parents, extensions of prayer, and their deepest wishes for my safety out in the world. My sisters gave me some Lip Smackers; my mother gave me a long gold chain with a medallion of Saint Christopher, the patron saint of safe travel; and my brother passed me a tin containing a small collection of his cut-off beard hair.

We were cuddled in the living room as a family when my dad reached behind him and pulled out a tiny box. "Happy birthday."

I smiled and took it from his outstretched hand, hoping I wouldn't have to fake liking whatever piece of jewellery he had bought me. Lifting the lid from the white box, I came face to face with my tiny scroll of wishes from almost four years earlier. The tiny scroll I'd hurled out the window into the frigid Winnipeg night.

He smiled in an "It's magic. I'm not telling" kind of way while I imagined him parking on one end of the Disraeli Bridge and walking along the narrow, slippery path, the headlights speeding by offering only moments of assistance to his one-man search party.

I imagined him searching for white on white, for a white of a different texture, in the darkness as the violent cold threatened to take his nose and eyelashes and fingertips. I imagined how after fifteen minutes, which is easily long enough to die, fully exposed, alone on the side of a bridge in forty below, he found my scroll of wishes.

I sat on our living room floor, surrounded by my family, and slowly unravelled the tiny scroll. The words, written in tiny all caps, said, *Get famous and make Paul love you.*

paul

a cheap facial

My parents bought a small cabin on Lake Winnipeg when we were kids. You could tell which bedroom was mine by a tiny hole in the wall, at waist level behind a set of drawers in the closet. I had hollowed it out with a steak knife. That hole looked into the spare room where my older brother's friends would sometimes change. I would squat in the darkness, hoping to catch a glimpse of some forbidden teenage-boy flesh. Usually giving my position away with a sneeze of projectile giggling before I got the chance to watch them lower their soggy bathing-suit bottoms.

It was winter. It was usually winter. It was New Year's Eve, the next New Year's Eve after Paul didn't fall in love with me at his house party. I was freshly sixteen. Paul, a couple friends of ours, and I had gone to the cabin for the weekend to ring in the new year.

I let my drunkenness inch me closer and closer to Paul. Thinking, *Maybe tonight. Maybe tonight he'll look over at me and I'll lean in and wipe his persistent eye goop away, then he'll run his boxy hands through my hair and kiss me with his thick pink lips.*

Midnight came and went. We yelled, "Happy New Year!" and hugged and jumped around the living room and did not kiss.

In the morning we began packing up to drive back to the city. We turned off the power, put out the fire, and collected the last of our crunchy teenage garbage. When I went into the bathroom to gather our towels, I came face to face with our weekend's shit and piss and some blood, frozen solid all the way up the toilet pipe and into the cheap plastic bowl.

I leaned over and pushed the busted flusher. It might as well have looked up at me and rolled its eyes as if to say, *No. Just no.*

I walked into the kitchen and collapsed onto one of the rubbery, yellow chairs and slowly, shamefully dialed my dad's number. My friends collected around me as my dad gave instructions for the necessary actions. I nodded, the palm of my hand pressed against my face as if I were receiving fatal news in the vein of *I'm so sorry. We did all we could. It was just too late.*

I put the phone down as my friends collectively asked, "What's happening?"

I stood up, filled the kettle with tap water that smelled like pennies, and put it on the coil stovetop. Pulling two big black garbage bags out of a cupboard, I explained the situation.

Paul started gagging as I described the scene in the bathroom and how I would have to take care of it. Some tiny, sick voice in my head whispered, *This is your chance, Hayley. This is your disgusting chance to save the day and take your rightful throne as Mrs. Paul forever and ever as long as you both shall live.*

I extended first one arm, then the other, asking him to duct tape the bags to the seam where sleeve becomes shoulder. I held my garbage-bag arms up like a surgeon about to walk into the operating room. Fingers extended to the sky, I said, "Kettle."

Paul grabbed the boiling kettle from the stovetop. Still gagging, he said, "Do you need" — (*barf noise*) — "help in there?" (*barf noise*).

I pulled my sweater over my face like a surgical mask and walked into the bathroom, shutting the door behind me.

As per my dad's instructions, I would have to pour, melt, and scoop until the frozen pipe was clear. I inched a bucket against the base of the toilet, then picked up the kettle. The boiling water hit the frozen shit and piss and blood, instantly producing steam that shot back up into my face like a cheap facial. I reached down with my garbage-bag arms, elbow deep, digging into the shit and piss and blood, thinking, *This is for Paul. Be strong for Paul.*

I emerged from the bathroom, pulling my sweater off my face. My friends clutched each other while Paul paced in the hallway with his hand over his mouth as if mumbling, *Why, God, why?*

I nodded and smiled. "It was a success. It's gonna need some rest for a while, but we should be in the clear."

They exhaled in unison.

Still gagging, Paul nodded in my direction and proceeded to not fall in love with me.

paul

the world in a moment

I stared up at the millions of stars as I gripped the sides of the rotting wooden table by the dock at our cabin, less than a year after our traumatic New Year's Eve. Our family bungalow looked a whole lot better upside down as I lay on my back, pushing my hands over my mouth and taking long, deep intentional breaths, Paul's face between my thighs.

This was Paul between my thighs. Paul. Paul, who I had wanted to touch since the moment I met him four years earlier, sitting against the wall outside of our rehearsal space at Manitoba Theatre for Young People, his black journal pressed against his knees and his dangling wallet chain resting beside him like an obedient pet. He had a level of confidence I found entirely seductive and equally unsettling. Even as a teenager he seemed to have lived this full life. He'd been in love already, had sex already, had a big, bad breakup already. His favourite pastimes included doing headstands to impress girls, injuring himself as a result of trying to impress girls, and sketching. Dressed all in black, he went to life-drawing classes, like a little man-boy, meticulously scribbling down the shapes of women twice his age. Cross-hatching arms and hips and breasts and mouths. He was weird and different, and I was half in love with him and half desperate to be him. To be as special as he was all on his own.

The warm summer air kissed my bare legs as I closed my eyes and tried with everything in me to just let go. Trying to let go might be an oxymoron. Letting go, in some ways, requires not trying. The more you try, the further you get from letting go, especially when you have a head between your legs for the first time.

I arched my back up and off the disintegrating table in a confused combination of pleasure and excitement and asking myself, *Am I gonna pee?* I dipped between bursts of laughter and gasps of pleasure and waves of … pain? My heart sped up ahead of me, grabbing my hand and nearly pulling my arm out of its socket, like a parent speedily dragging a child through a Boxing Day sale.

It's confusing to feel your body heading to a destination but having no idea what that destination looks like. You've never been there before, and while, yeah, you've heard people talk about it, there is really no way to pack for it before you arrive. Like, do I bring sweaters? A bathing suit? Runners? Will I have time to read?

I turned my head to the left and saw a small stack of stones and shells, harvested from the shoreline and set out to dry earlier that day. I had been in love with Paul since the day I met him. I had been in love with Paul since I pounced on him in the parking lot behind our theatre school, planting my first kiss on his unsuspecting face, then sprinting away into the night like a crazy person. That kiss was followed by Paul's saying he only saw me as a friend. That sweet, sad, surprise ambush of a kiss was followed by two full years of his being just friends, while I quietly schemed and peacocked and waited for him to look over and realize he was in love with me.

I wish I could tell you what it was that made Paul suddenly interested in me after years of knowing I had feelings for him. The truth is it could have been anything. Maybe it was a specific track on one of the dozen or so mix CDs I made him over the years, or maybe it was some scene I did in theatre school that made him view me in a different way, or maybe it was my short-lived crush on Jude from high school that gave Paul the opportunity to feel what not having my undying attention felt like.

I hesitated to reach down and push my hands against Paul's head, to gingerly slip my fingers into his soft, brown tendrils in the darkness, like that line of touch hadn't been bridged yet. My brain didn't yet know how to tell my hand to do the thing it wanted to do. The neural pathway had not yet been carved out.

I realize people try hard to live in the moment. I think I have the exact opposite issue. I build entire worlds in a moment. I live in the complete power of a touch or look or word. Everything that ever happened to me leading up to that moment dissolves and I am only the puddle at your feet. There is no aftermath; there is no potential for an unfortunate end. There is nothing but your hands and my skin.

Paul had a similar ailment. He, too, did not consider potential outcomes or unfortunate ends. Over the following decade he would continue to dive into these moments, moments opening like random and unexpected portals into an alternate reality where we were lovers. He dove fully into his momentary and fleeting romantic feelings for me, always reappearing as a friend on the other side, leaving me with recurring emotional motion sickness and cardiovascular whiplash.

cye

grand gestures

Cye was my first real boyfriend. He was insanely talented, and I was insanely twenty.

He gave me a key to his second-floor Toronto apartment. The apartment on top of a cheese store and next to a bar that played shitty funk every Thursday night.

The apartment we killed fifty-six mice in one summer, keeping a tally in knife marks gouged on the back door. Emptying our traps, enjoying tiny bursts of sadistic satisfaction every time we caught a new one.

The apartment where he would make me popcorn, his ador-able belly jiggling as he shook the pot to disperse the salt evenly. Where we would sing the theme song to *SVU* while eating sushi on his living room floor.

The apartment where we fucked for the first time. Where he figured out how to make me cum regularly, then affectionately titled the move the Shuffle.

The apartment where he hog-tied me. Tying my ankles together and my wrists together, then tying my ankles and my wrists together behind my back.

The apartment where we tried anal for the first time. Where he moved just a little too fast and I burst into tears. I burst into tears like turning on a light, a full and immediate sob with the flick of a switch.

The apartment where I slept tucked into his giant house-body on a single bed for three years.

The apartment I essentially broke into, like a crazy person, after one of our three breakups, to leave a painting I had made for him of the New York City skyline. A painting I made entirely of pinprick-sized dots of paint. A painting I made in exchange for sleeplessness. He was knocked out on the couch when I broke in to leave it for him. He thought I was a burglar. I placed the painting on his computer and inched backward out of the room muttering, "Hi, fuck, sorry, go back to sleep, just leaving some-thing … go back to sleep … fuck. Sorry."

The apartment where I eventually begged him to give us another chance as he stood over me on the couch yelling, "I don't love you anymore."

My language of love with Cye was grand gestures.

I tend to go way over the top with men that I am just not sure love me. I'll secretly front large bills, spending money I don't have. I'll spend six hours making a cake, weeks planning a trip. I'll do home renovations and I'll wait all afternoon for the air-conditioning technician to come fix the unit so the object of my affection doesn't have to miss the Beach Boys concert he has tickets to.

I spent six months on Cye's twenty-ninth birthday gift, a personalized cookbook of my mother's family recipes. I spent six months going through her old handwritten recipes and typing them out. I hired a stylist and makeup artist and got his photographer friend to photograph a cover. I got another one of his friends to design the font and put together the layout. Then I printed two copies of the book, one for him and one for my mother.

For his thirtieth, I needed to do something huge. Something I could plant in his memory as the thing that no other woman had ever done for him. A way to solidify myself in his heart and mind forever, regardless of what happened between us down the line. A way to win.

Cye moved to Canada on a full music scholarship when he was sixteen. In all the years he'd lived in Canada, he'd never been back to Italy to see his mother and grandmother, and they had not been able to afford to come see him.

I managed to slip onto his computer one afternoon when he was out. I searched through his emails looking for his mother's name, obsessively checking over my shoulder to make sure he didn't walk in and catch me.

Hi Francesca. It's Hayley. How are you? I want to surprise fly you to Canada for Cye's 30th birthday, I typed.

She wrote me back the following morning in weepy broken English.

I spent three weeks applying for an international visa on her behalf, compiling my father's tax documents in support of her application. By the morning of her flight, she still hadn't received her approval notice. I was receiving her traumatized emails as she sat at her window waiting for the mailman, like Cye used to wait in vain on their doorstep for his father to take him out for the day.

The mailman finally pulled up. I imagine he walked to her door in slow motion, with long, flowing, silver hair like Dumbledore, one glistening white envelope in his hand and a sudden gust of wind blowing his locks back.

Visa documents included. Please staple into your passport …

I cuddled into Cye's giant, warm house-body listening to the drunks on College Street and panicking about his mother, praying that she'd caught her connecting flight and was not sleeping on the cold, hard floor of the Zurich airport. Most likely using some kind of scarf as a blanket.

We woke up the next morning in the exact position we'd gone to sleep in. It's what happens when you're sharing a single bed with a man who's six foot five. You take spooning to a whole new level — like runny broth in a spoon, you take up only the space that he's hollowed out for scooping, lest you spill everywhere.

She was set to arrive in Toronto in the late afternoon, so a small group of his close friends and I took over a few of the patio tables at a little café on a corner near his place. I got a phone call from my dad, who had arranged for a driver to pick up Francesca from the airport. We sat and ate while I tried very hard to be unaffected, relaxed, chill.

Fifteen minutes later, I got a call from the driver telling me they were pulling up. My heart pounding, my hands sweating, I looked at one of his best friends and mouthed the word *now*.

He lifted his coat and covered Cye's head.

I jumped over the side of the patio and ran to meet the black car pulling up. The door shot open. This sweet, exhausted, overwhelmed little woman tumbled out of the back seat the way a piece of furniture does when it's no longer being held in by the structural support of the door. She was wearing flowing pants, maroon boots, a black feathered scarf, and turquoise reading glasses on one of those necklace tether things pressed against her chest.

She hugged me like I was taking over for the car door. Like she was using my body to remain upright. I pulled her pink suitcase out of the trunk and pointed toward the patio.

Trying to avoid knocking over everything in her path, she dodged waiters and tables and crossed legs like they were an obstacle course. Too overwhelmed to sit beside Cye, she jumped up on the wooden bench, reached down, and grabbed his hands.

His friend slowly pulled the jacket off Cye's face. Cye looked up at her and gasped the way you do when you've narrowly avoided falling from some great height.

Inches from him for the first time in fourteen years, she reached out her hands and placed them on his cheeks.

We all disappeared.

He was her son.

She was his mother.

They cried, their hands running over each other's faces, collecting tears with their fingertips. Tracing the lines and the greys and the scars that had sprouted up in their time apart.

And I felt proud.

And I felt sure that all this joy would overshadow any pain or struggle or conflict we would ever face. Like I had successfully bandaged the many parts of our relationship that didn't work at all, with one single, grand gesture.

ben ∿ cye

why i left ben

Generally, when a man is immediately interested in me, I question what he's even interested in. Before he knows me, before he knows what I like and dislike, before he knows that I could live exclusively off a variety of nut butters and that anime gives me nightmares.

Turns out I believe in loving at first sight but definitely not in being loved at first sight.

After the second of our three breakups, I was at a party conveniently located down the street from Cye. Just close enough so it was impossible for me to not feel like he was peering over my shoulder, watching me flirt with the sweet, flopsy-haired, permanent-morning-faced Ben. My eyes met Ben's over the drum kit, where he was sloppily smashing a symbol. He smiled and smashed and smashed and smiled.

I had spent the few months since Cye's birthday applying makeup to his corpse. Trying to paint life onto a relationship that was very much dead. Trying to dab pink blush onto his cold, lifeless cheeks, smearing my MAC lipstick on his chilled blue lips. Trying to prop him up at the dinner table, wedge a wine glass into his mummifying fingers, and fill the sides of his mouth with packing Styrofoam to mimic a smile.

I leaned against the chipped eggshell paint on the wall just outside the room Ben was drumming in. I waited to hear the beat stop, notifying me that Ben was unwedging himself from the drum kit to come find me. Standing in front of me in the hall, he clasped his arms behind his back and asked if I needed a drink. I rolled my lower lip between my fingers, grinning and suddenly hyperaware of my mouth.

My pocket buzzed and buzzed. I ignored it. It stopped, then it buzzed and buzzed again.

I pressed my annoyed and now worried palm against my phone and pried myself away from Ben's sparkling hazel eyes. I slapped on a fake smile and inched up the stairs between a girl crying, a couple making out, and a guy yelling, "Happy New Year!" though it was mid-May.

I sat on the toilet with my hot phone pressed to my ear. Cye yelled and cried and begged as I apologized for who knows what and pleaded for who knows what and then eventually agreed to leave the party and walk to his place.

I found Ben downstairs and told him I had to go. I gave him a quick, vague Coles Notes summary, explaining the flailing ex down the street.

He walked me to Cye's door. Suggestively brushing up against me on our charged moonlit walk. Standing under Cye's bedroom window, we kissed for the first time.

He leaned in.

He leaned down.

He tenderly wrapped his fingers around the back of my head, pushing my hair against the nape of my neck, and relaxed his lips into mine.

I felt this wave of love.

This totally obvious connection.

This kiss that we both knew was the start of something.

I looked up into Ben's eyes, wanting to pitch a tent in them. Wanting to nuzzle into a sleeping bag under a cool, clear, starry night sky and fall asleep to the smell of a freshly extinguished campfire.

Then I went inside and fucked Cye.

It was Ben's sister's birthday a few weeks later. I spent the evening at his family's house. We popped champagne on their tiny back patio and threw pink and blue and yellow homemade confetti into the smoggy, grey Toronto sky.

My phone vibrated against my hip as I ran my index finger over Ben's plate, collecting the last of his pastel-peach birthday-cake icing.

My pocket buzzed and buzzed. I ignored it. It stopped, then it buzzed and buzzed again.

I pressed my annoyed and now a bit worried palm against my phone and tiptoed up to the bathroom, leaving all the joy and celebration behind me.

"Cye. What's up? Are you okay?"

Crying and panicking and drunk, he begged me to come over. I said no over and over and over, until I couldn't anymore. Until it felt like the only way out was in.

Cye's front door was open. I anxiously walked up his long staircase, calculating his level of drunkenness by the sounds his body made as he clumsily paced around his living room. I came around the corner to find him on his rolling chair, drinking white wine straight out of the bottle.

He saw me and burst into tears. He closed his eyes and motioned for me to come over to him. He leaned his head into my chest, running his hands up the backs of my legs. Squeezing my thighs like I was made of some substance that would vaporize if he released it.

"Please stay the night," he said.

"No," I said.

"Please, just lie down with me."

"No," I said.

We played this yes–no game for a while as my phone vibrated against my hip with concerned texts from Ben, who was circling Cye's block on his bike — though I didn't find out he was doing that until much later.

Eventually, it felt like the only way out was in. I said, "I'll lie down with you for twenty minutes, then I'm going home."

With his arms wrapped around me, he walked me into his tiny bedroom. Lying down he said, "I need to taste you. Please."

I said no.

Then I said no again.

Then I said fine.

He moved his head down my body, over my chest, kissing my soft, imperfect tummy and half crying. He put his mouth on me.

I put my hands over my eyes, catching glimpses of the smoggy night sky through the cracks in my fingers. Imagining the homemade pink and blue and yellow confetti filling the grey Toronto night, like it had a half an hour earlier.

He lifted his head from between my legs and said, "I want you to taste me. Please."

I said no.

Then I said no again.

Then I said fine.

Feeling like the only way out was in, I pushed him into my mouth.

As soon as he finished, I got up to go to the bathroom. I locked the door and messaged Ben. *I'm about to leave. Can I please come back?*

Of course, you can.

I walked back down Cye's long hallway. I leaned against his door and said, "I'm gonna go home. I wanna go home."

He begged a few more times for me to stay, then shifted into "Are you actually going home?"

I lied and said yes.

He walked me outside and hailed a cab, then gave the driver my address. I waited until Cye had disappeared from the rear-view mirror to tell the cabby to reroute and take me to Ben.

As the cab pulled up, Ben came outside to meet me on his front step. Exhausted, I collapsed into his chest. Silently, he held me there.

We walked up his carpeted staircase, careful not to wake the rest of his sleeping family.

Trying very hard not to cry, I stood beside his bed. He pulled back his sheets, flipped over a pillow, laid my head down on the cool cotton, and asked for nothing. He asked me for no explanation, for no series of events, no account of the last few lost hours. He simply pressed his palm firmly over my fluttering heart and whispered, "Just breathe, Hayley." He kissed my cheek and held me while my phone buzzed and buzzed and buzzed at the foot of his bed.

This night paved the way for the rest of that summer. This pull and pressure I felt to go back to Cye. This emotional blackmailing that he called love. This emotional blackmailing that I, too, called love.

Cye's forceful and aggressive get-Hayley-to-love-me campaign made Ben's love unrecognizable to me. Because they couldn't both be love. Two things that looked and felt so different couldn't both be love.

And I made the fatal mistake of assigning more value to the thing that was harder to have. As if holding something that's searing your skin off increases its value. I stopped knowing how to be happy with happy when it was being held up next to painful and difficult and desperate, and I started feeling guilty.

Guilty for letting someone new make me feel good.

Guilty for that night.

Eventually, I decided I wasn't worthy of Ben. I deemed his love for me less valuable, less real, because it was given with such abandon, and I decided he was better off without me.

I decided Cye needed me more, and I decided to rate my worth on need alone.

ben ᔐ cye

bad choices

Ben and I stood in the doorway of my rented house on Brock. The house where I slept in the attic with the ceiling that had bubbled from two solid weeks of Toronto autumn rain.

I liked that ceiling.

I like having something secretly decomposing somewhere in my life. Some ticking time bomb that eventually requires all my attention. Something that gives me full permission to cancel every plan on no notice.

I unknowingly set up these ticking time bombs in my life. I do it by picking the wrong men, ignoring injuries, hiding rotting leftovers. I do it by quietly, unintentionally, setting myself up for failure. Perhaps as a way to ensure I'll have some other force to blame when shit inevitably goes sour.

"I love you," he said. "I love you."

We stood there, Ben's flopsy brown hair in my hands, and his permanent morning face, plump and pink and warm, pressed against mine. The fractured morning light spilling between our connected lips, our kisses salty from our fresh tears.

I wrapped my arms around him, clutching his denim button-up in my fists. I let his words spin around me, knowing I felt the same and knowing I couldn't keep him.

"I love you, too," I whispered, my lips pressed against his ear.

We held each other as he leaned down to wrap his arms around my lower back, encouraging my chin onto his shoulder.

Then he said something I didn't totally understand at first. He said, "He's here."

"What? Who's here?"

Ben pulled away from me, suddenly green, suddenly cold, suddenly eight years old. I followed his frozen gaze, letting it direct me out the front door and to the gate at the end of the path leading to the street.

There *he* was.

Cye, my six-foot-five ex. The ex whose house I had just left. The ex I had just told, thirty minutes earlier, that I was going to give him another shot after he had ripped my heart out earlier that summer. After he had stood over me in his mouse-infested apartment, yelling, "I don't love you anymore."

I wanted to disappear. I wanted run backward in time, just a few years back to a time when I was entirely undesired. To a time when I was certain no one would ever want me.

I suddenly felt green and cold and eight years old, entirely unequipped to handle the love of these two men.

Ben turned and walked out the front door. I kept his denim shirt in my palm until his distance pulled it from me.

"I'm so sorry," I whispered to the back of his beautiful head, unable to burst into tears the way I wanted to, having to curb my sadness for the sake of my ex at the end of the path.

They met for a second at the swinging gate. Cye stood like a statue with his bike only slightly to one side of the entrance. He stood looking up at the house, as my dewy, morning-faced Ben squeezed past him.

I watched Ben's flopsy brown hair as he walked over to his little blue car. I watched him drive away, softly comforted by the fact that he deserved someone way better than me and that I certainly did not deserve him.

Cye leaned his bike against the fence and walked up to the house. He walked slowly, with his head down as if in a funeral procession. He sat down on the stairs and put his face in his hands. I let the glass door swing shut and sat down beside him.

I looked up, not totally sure who I was crying for.

We sat, suddenly aware of how loud the wind was and knowing that this horrible moment would eventually end our relationship for good.

ben

the one that got away

With some breakups, you see it coming. Over coffee one morning, you spot the ominous hooded Ghost of Breakups Future lingering at the edge of your street. You top off your coffee or start peeling a banana and pretend not to notice him inching closer. You look at the pile of laundry in the corner and hope he'll realize he's got the wrong house. Like, you haven't heard the couple next door having sex for a while, so surely, he read your address wrong. Surely, he's going to walk in, notice that your relationship is perfectly intact, and realize what a silly mistake he's made. You'll all laugh and he'll bashfully place his hand on his fleshless cheek and offer up his sincerest apologies. You'll pack him a bag of carrots in room-temperature raisin water for the road and jokingly say, "Hope to never see you again." You and your beloved will stand side by side, holding your warm coffee cups, waving to him in unison through the window as he strolls next door to ruin someone else's life.

Ben and I had gotten back together, and we'd been good. Like, really good. We'd managed to recover from the time I'd ripped his heart out of his chest the previous summer. We had nurtured the growth of all the trust and love and consistency in the almost-year we'd shared. We'd gone on trips with my family, with his family. We'd had dinners and walks and parties. We'd laughed and cried and felt lucky to have each other. And perhaps it was knowing that we had managed to get to the other side of my really hurting him that made me certain we could recover from anything. Like, we'd already done the hard thing.

We woke up in my new, cozy third-floor Toronto apartment a week before our one-year anniversary. He was lying beside me, his perfect flopsy brown curls poking out of a heap of blankets. I reached over and ran my fingers through his hair, then pulled the sheets back far enough to press my face into the back of his neck.

I mean, just kill me. The smell of his body. His thick, musky, warm, tender body.

I pulled myself out of bed, not knowing it would be the last time I'd ever be that close to him. I filled the kettle and placed it on the stove as he sluggishly emerged from my room and sat down at my kitchen table, fully dressed. I noticed his tangled expression as that hooded figure appeared on my balcony, looking out over Toronto, his hands in his pockets.

"You okay?" I asked.

"I don't know. I'm confused," Ben said.

"About what? About me?"

"Maybe, yeah. And I just don't know what I'm doing with my life."

The Ghost of Breakups Future creaked open the door and quietly sat across from Ben, as if to say, *Shit. Sorry. Didn't mean to interrupt. Sorry.*

"Do you still love me?" I said.

"I don't know," Ben said.

"Well. Maybe you should go figure that out somewhere that isn't my kitchen."

Tears filled his eyes as he pulled on his sneakers in what felt like super-slow motion. Then he left. I sat on the floor with my back pressed against the door and listened to his steps get farther and farther and quieter and quieter, then gone.

And that was kind of it.

We spoke again, of course. But the moment he left my home, he became more and more sure that he didn't love me in the way I loved him, and unlike almost every other man in my entire romantic life, he never wavered. He never gave me a second of hope. We never fucked again. He never dropped me a bread-crumb or a *maybe in the future*. Or anything. He made a decision and he stuck to it.

At the time it felt devastatingly cruel, but now it feels almost noble. It feels like a reflection of his actual care for me. In the sea of men who have had no problem torturing me for weeks, months, years, he just didn't.

All I wanted was for him to repurpose me in some way that would allow me to keep loving him. All I wanted was for him to not know that it was a no. To let me keep the door open a crack, just enough to make it virtually impossible for me to move on.

He didn't do that.

tal

giving in

Every time Tal did something inexcusable and I didn't let it instigate the end of my involvement with him, it pushed my tolerance a little further and it gave him a little more permission to get a little bit darker.

At this point, I'd been living in his place for six months since he pulled me out of the dude house. I was settled into our dysfunction, bronzed in secrecy at his side. The room I was meant to be sleeping in at his place was almost exclusively used for storage as I begged him to keep our affair quiet from the rest of the studio, utterly ashamed of the reality I had casually woken up in.

I would curl up beside him in his piss-coloured North Hollywood apartment, watching movies and pretending I was okay. Then roll over just enough so he could Skype with Molly in Canada before bed without her seeing me in the frame beside him. I'd watch her look at him, whispering good night like lovers do, and I'd see his live reflection on the computer screen, and I'd believe that guy somehow, just like she did.

I barely understood how I got in so deep that it was near-impossible for me to imagine a way out.

I called us dysfunctional. I called us challenging, complicated, confusing, because I know where to put those things. It's comforting to give something a name, because nameless things are new and unknown and terrifying.

My eyes caught on a tiny red light at the foot of the bed.

I squinted to make out his computer, the screen open, dark, and the red light quietly filming us.

He ran his hands up my thighs and grabbed my waist hard to flip me toward the side of the bed. Facing the window, he knelt behind me and pulled my hair back with one hand, pushing the other into my lower back.

I thought, *Don't panic. Just ask about it tomorrow when he's gone.*

He flew to Canada the next morning to be with Molly for a week. I waited until he left the apartment, then texted, *Hey, where is that video from last night? I wanna watch it. ;)*

It felt wiser to play along.

It felt wiser to not corner the dog.

I deleted it, he wrote.

I didn't believe him.

I nervously pulled out his computer and involuntarily scanned the room for other unexpected blinking red lights. I typed *mov* into the search box. I scanned the results: dozens of rehearsal videos, shirtless guitar-playing videos, music-video footage. Then I stumbled onto a file dated a few days earlier, time-stamped 11:10 a.m., a tiny thumbnail of his bedroom lit up by the stupid studio lights he used instead of lamps. I knew it wasn't the video I was looking for; I knew it wasn't of me.

I double-clicked.

Sitting cross-legged on his bed, I watched his naked body enter the screen.

I spotted my journal on the bedside table in the shot, my cup of tea, my iPhone charger.

He came up to the camera, adjusted the frame, then walked out of the picture. I heard him move down the hallway and open the front door.

He re-entered the room with this beautiful woman. He started stripping her clothes off as she said, "I don't get a hello?"

"Nope," he said as he continued stripping her.

I paused the video for a second to check my phone to see where I was that day. I had left for brunch with a friend thirty minutes before it was taken. He had kissed me at the front door. I had jumped into my friend's car and driven away to eat fucking gluten-free toast while he fucked a stranger in my still-warm ass print on the bed.

I sat on his sheets, my hands over my mouth, shaking and sobbing and rewatching the video over and over. Unable to look away, like witnessing a terrifying car accident. Pausing the video in the frames of him cumming, of her cumming, of the quiet somethings whispered between them.

I started flashing between the present moment and the previous evening, when he was filming me without my permission. In a shot of panic-fuelled adrenalin, I started looking through every box in his closet. I pulled out old hard drives and USBs, feverishly hunting through them, creating a circle of material around me on the bed like I was preparing for a seance. I plugged in hard drive after hard drive, scanning and searching for nakedness — nakedness that seemed like an agreement between only Tal and Tal's computer.

I found nothing but the girl from a few days earlier.

He was going to be in Canada for a week. Before he got back, I found a cheap car rental, tossed it onto my buckling Visa, and loaded all of my stuff into its trunk.

Before he'd left, I had agreed to pick him up from the airport in his car. I took one last look around his place, making sure there was nothing of mine left, then drove to LAX.

He texted me when he got out of the terminal, and I pulled up to get him, my stomach sinking as he tossed his bag into the trunk and jumped into the front seat, leaning in to kiss my neck. A peck like a flick with your index finger, short and percussive. We small-talked for a few minutes: just how terrible Canada was, how much it was over with Molly, his regular campaign of trying to convince me they were at the tail end of their relationship.

Eventually, I just launched into it. "Listen, I found the video on your computer of you and that girl from a couple weeks ago. It's fine, but I can't stay with you anymore. I've moved all my stuff out. I'm leaving tonight."

He tried to convince me it was an old video. I stopped him calmly. "No, it's not. The video is dated, and my stuff is on the bedside table in the shot. It's fine. I just can't stay with you anymore."

When we got back to his place, I climbed out of his car in silence, passed him the keys, and climbed into mine.

Fifteen minutes into my drive, I received a panicked phone call. "Hayley, you have to come back. I have to go to the hospital."

Without thinking, I turned around and sped back to his place, tossing aside my escape plan. I found him curled up on the floor of his apartment, crying and moaning, his hands pressed against his stomach, writhing in pain. I knelt beside him, draped his arm over my shoulder, lifted him up, and walked him out to his car, then helped him into the passenger seat.

In the emergency room, he hobbled over to the counter to fill out the paperwork, then sat down beside me on the cold, hard plastic seat, snuggling up against my arm like a wounded puppy, being affectionate in a way he almost never was. Nuzzling into my shoulder, he lifted my hand and placed it on his head, encouraging my fingers to comfort him.

We stayed like this for six hours. At about 5:00 a.m., he walked back up to the counter, got a piece of paper from the nurse, and returned to me, saying we could leave. He never saw a doctor.

He exhaustedly climbed into the car and we drove back to his place. As we pulled up to his parking garage, he said, "Hayley, it's almost six. Just come in and get some sleep for a few hours. Leave later."

I didn't trust him, but I got out of the car. I walked down the hallway, terrified he would look into his room, notice something slightly out of place, and figure out that I had ripped the space apart in a wave of pure panic and fear. I turned left into the spare bedroom I was meant to be sleeping in and let him turn right, alone, into his.

A couple seconds later he walked into the spare room and approached me to give me a hug. "I'm gonna sleep in here. Okay?" he said. He wrapped his arms around me and pulled me tightly against him.

With my face pressed against his ear, I said, "I just need to sleep."

He bent his knees and began running his hands up my legs; up my dress; over my soft, imperfect stomach; over my breasts, growling in my ear like he always did.

I looked over his shoulder and found myself in the mirror behind him. I watched my slow, steady tears flood through my eyelashes, blurring my reflection, then clearing it with a single blink. He kissed my pink cheeks as I let go and gave into him, letting him move me to the bed and lie down on top of me.

He finished and I did not leave.

diego

hide in my suitcase

"Hi, Hayley."

I looked up to find Diego. Just inches from me, tall and dark, looking down at me with his disarming eye contact. His stupidly handsome face, imperfect teeth, and a tiny bump on the bridge of his nose that I would later find out he was certain was cancer.

It wasn't.

I sort of knew Diego. I knew him as one of Paul's classmates. I knew him as that few-years-older-than-me guy I'd made casual eye contact with over the years, while following Paul around his theatre school.

It was winter in Montreal. I was eighteen, in town visiting Paul during one of our we're-just-friends chapters. We arrived at an impossibly cool house party. Impossibly cool people sprawled over couches on Moroccan carpeted floors, perched on tables, and smoking stubby hand-rolled cigarettes out of the living room windows.

At eighteen, this was a snapshot of adulthood for me. A sexy glimpse of what my life might look like, the kinds of people I might get to be surrounded by. The kinds of opinions I might get to develop. The kind of person I might get to become.

Paul got flagged down by some beautiful, artsy wisp of a woman and left me to fend for myself. I walked to the kitchen, weaving in and out of groups of stunning men and women, few of whom I knew, all of whom I imagined were just coming from a workshop or book launch or gallery opening. I reached into the fridge and threw back a beer, needing to quickly diffuse my self-consciousness.

The key to not appearing lonely and uncomfortable is busyness. Stay busy. Stack cups, reorganize the counter, tear all the skin off your right thumb, starting at the cuticles and working your way down.

Diego walked into the kitchen and pulled a beer out of the fridge with a confidence that made me wonder if it was his house. Then he leaned against the counter beside me as if we'd planned to meet there.

"So, Jen has been sleeping with Marco, over there. Marco and El broke up like six months ago. He lost his shit and like fifteen pounds. Arwen dropped out in first year — actually I'm surprised she's here. Oh, and T, by the bathroom, he's had a crush on you since you came to visit two years ago.... But I mean, who hasn't?"

He tossed out that last one without turning to look at me. He let me receive his expertly delivered line in the safety of my unpenetrated bubble.

In a room of at least fifty gorgeous, creative weirdos, he didn't for a second make me feel like he'd rather be talking to any of them. He settled into our conversation like he was being graded on it.

With each passing beer, our proper counter lean became more of an informal slunk-down kitchen-floor sit. We laughed and talked and drank, riding out the last couple hours of the party as people scattered back into the night.

Eventually, Paul resurfaced and went to find our coats in the now small heap of coats and scarves at the front door, and I turned to say good night to my Costa Rican kitchen saviour.

He smiled, revealing his perfectly imperfect teeth, and said, "What's your email address?" I nervously rattled it off to him. "Remind me to tell you a secret," he said.

Walking out into the asshole that is Montreal winter, I looked back over my shoulder to see him still leaning against the counter, warm and drunk and smiling at me.

I flew back to Winnipeg the next morning: "Yes, parents, Montreal was fun, and no, Dad, I didn't attempt to speak French with anyone."

I weaseled my way down to our communal computer in the basement and logged into my email to find Diego's mysterious, mature, experienced, worldly, sophisticated, promising name in my inbox. He wrote,

> *My secret: Like the evening, it's now part of this lovely world. This lovely world is made up of memories which combined with an empty kitchen can be lethal.*
>
> *The secret: Quite simple. Last night I meant to say, now I'm gonna make up stories around and about you. There. It's a little tendency I have which you said you share. The secret's out.*
>
> *… To a common ground, found in the mess of millions of blind, sloppy nights.*

I exhaled. I read his words over and over, my elbows propped on the desk in front of the keyboard and my hands pressed against my hot cheeks. I pressed reply and began to dizzily piece together a response. I wrote,

> *Oh, there you are. I've been writing all day; a song I think I would like to play for you sometime. Sitting in front of you sometime. You've become my overnight excuse to create. Thank you for that. Hope to hear from you soon.*

Our emails snowballed quickly. Suddenly, wherever I could get my hands on a computer became the most important place in my life. He wrote,

> *To kiss you … I imagine it would be like drinking water or saying hello in its simplicity, its naturality. Like it was meant to happen in the course of the universe since the beginning of time. But it would also be like touching fire or swimming deep inside the ocean in its inexplicable beauty and sweet sweet danger. Thank you thank you for adding yourself to my life because I wake up wondering what you're doing. And I find that very comforting.*

I was an eighteen-year-old virgin.

I fucking died.

We moved from one email a day to two, to three, to three plus real mail, to real mail plus real phone calls, and eventually to real phone calls plus real plans.

He was working on a play in Montreal with his classmates when he wrote,

I think you should hide in my suitcase when the final
curtain falls. That way, you can jump out when I get to
Chicago, follow me to the big city then back to Toronto,
then to, wherever you want to go (not kidding) not
kidding, not kidding. Or, what about Europe?

diego

i'm fucked

Montreal was cool and romantic, quiet and cinematic, like the opening of the original cartoon version of *101 Dalmatians*. Fashionable dogs being walked by their look-alike owners, and young lovers brushing against each other under the soft orange street lights.

I'd catch glimpses of Diego's hands brushing his dark curls out of his face or adjusting the collar on his jacket and think, *I know those hands but I don't know those hands. Those fingers have been running over a keyboard somewhere in the world typing two months of poetry at me.*

He had written,

Where did this come from?
Why? I care less and less every day.
I question it just long enough to see the mystery and
then leave it alone. I've lived through the most
unimaginable adventures and the one thing I've
learned from it is that it's so easy to meet people who
don't move you. And that's never questioned.
It's a part of my daily life and I don't mean that in an
arrogant way. I mean it honestly. So meeting someone
who shakes your foundations, restructures your
heart and its pace and shatters a couple windows and
opens your eyes WIDE to let yellow light come
in … that I don't question … I indulge it actually. I
indulge in you at the moment.

The more I watched him, the more my body melted beneath me, leaving a grinning puddle on the chilly cobblestone. I dragged my rolling suitcase through the quiet evening streets, hoping I hadn't forgotten to pack anything for our month of travelling.

We got back to his place, an inviting narrow red door leading to an even narrower staircase up to the second floor of a townhouse. He walked in ahead of me. By the time I'd dropped my bags and entered the dining room, he had lit two candles, which flickered over a perfectly set table.

He looked over his shoulder and smiled at me from the kitchen, where he had already begun pulling prepped ingredients out of the fridge. Taking a sharp knife, he halved an avocado. He filled it with some sort of tuna mixture and lovingly placed a piece of cheese on top, then bent down to the oven to give it a quick broil.

I tried hard to quiet the voice in my head that whispered, *Do you have any idea how many calories are in that?… Hayley, we can't …*

the cheese, the avocado! If you eat it, you get fat and he won't love you....
Though, if you don't eat it, you're rude and he won't love you. Fuck.

Forcing an easygoing, I'll-eat-anything kind of smile, I sat at the table while he talked to me from the kitchen. I tried hard to shake myself back into the moment while quietly calculating the caloric price tag of getting him to like me. I watched his body dip in and out of view behind the kitchen counter, purposefully chopping and garnishing all for me.

About fifteen minutes later, he walked out of the kitchen, flicked on the white Christmas lights that were wound around a pillar in the middle of the living room, and joined me at the table. The meal was a blur. I stared into his perfect face, too nervous to say much. I leaned into his age and experience, letting him cradle the conversation like a confident parent.

As we ate our final bites, he picked up his wine to make a toast. I lifted my glass and smiled, holding his perfect eyes in perfect eye contact. We watched each other distort through the glasses as we drank.

As if in a John Hughes movie, he stood up, reached his hand out, slid the plates and napkins and food to one side with his forearm, wrapped his fingers around the nape of my neck, and kissed me from across the table. As we inched off the side of our chairs, our lips still connected, he pulled me over to the pillar and leaned me against the soft white Christmas lights.

With his arm wrapped around my lower back, his fingers in my hair, his lips on my neck, he walked me toward the bedroom.

> *I am barely in my head now.*
> *I am my goosebumps.*
> *I am my pink cheeks.*
> *I am my closed eyes.*
> *I am my open mouth.*
> *And we're walking to his room now.*

And I'm lying on his bed now.
And my shirt is still on but my pants are pulled off now.
And he's kissing my neck and my cheeks and I'm
staring at the ceiling with my hand on the back of
his neck now.
And he's hovering over me. His body pressed to mine
and I can feel him against my thigh and he's pausing,
looking into my eyes.
And it hurts for a second, then it doesn't. And I don't
know what to do with my body other than receive him.
So I am still and open and warm.

And maybe it was because we'd released something that had
been so built up for so many weeks, but the next morning I
woke up and the bed was empty, and he was in the other room
and he was busy. I guess his mind told his hands to be full because
if they were occupied and active, then perhaps I would notice
there was no space for me in them.

He was deflated and different. Nervous maybe. Like the
thing we really shared was this precious anticipation, and the second it was gone we were strangers again. And I thought, *Maybe*
this reality will go away if I don't look at it. If I just continue living in
the last two months of emails. If I actively avoid his body and face and
subtle dismissive expressions. If I take the book I printed of our months
of emails into the bathroom and reread his words while he's just outside
the door.

I read them over and over. Missing someone that didn't exist
anymore. Not for me at least. Just three days before, he'd written,

I was left standing on a corner in Montreal as
you and three of my friends got in a cab. And the
last thing I saw was you turning around in the back seat
to look at me. That night I came home and I thought

of you more than I rationally should have. And the
next day I called you at Pascal's but there was no
answer. Then I thought, "What am I doing?
This is weird." And deep inside of my head
someone said, well, you're — well, it's Hayley.
And I wanted to tell you, that I now incessantly and
softly, really really softly take your left strap in my
fingers and hike it up back into place and then
continue the sliding ride up your neck and into your
hair till I have enough grip to guide your lips over to
mine.

My memory is too good. I was fucked.

me

smaller

It's hard to find the exact moment an eating disorder begins. In almost every way, she's separate from you at first. She's a sort of body double. She looks like you and sounds like you and knows everything about you. In almost every way, she is born as someone separate, then eventually nuzzles into your skin like a tick until she's a part of you.

She starts in the form of passing comments. Passing comments that aren't even meant to hurt. She is born out of "Wow, you're tall for your age," or "You just have big bones," or "Hayley, let's get you on the ground tier of the pyramid." She is birthed out of the moment when you're eight and a babysitter casually leans over and says, "As long as you can touch each of your fingers to your thumb around your wrist, you aren't fat."

These passing words and echoing phrases hide inside of you and fester until you are reunited with a mirror, and then, all of a sudden, you notice you are really tall and you are significantly thicker than Mauri Rosenberg, your current best friend, who is easily the smallest person in your class. And now, suddenly, it's *your* voice saying the things. Your voice is calling you too thick and too tall and way bigger than Mauri as you look down and realize you're clicking your fingers to your thumb around your wrist, just checking.

And just like that, she is born, and you will spend the rest of your life fighting her off. You will wrestle her out of the bedroom and kick her out of the shower. You will beg her to stop tampering with your relationships and ask her again, politely, to please stop touching your jeans and, like, "Girl, can't you make plans of your own? Do you have to come with me on every fucking date I have?"

I was in a choir in Winnipeg for almost six years, from twelve to seventeen. We would rehearse every Wednesday in a high-school gym at the other end of the city. I was not a great choir member. I guess I sort of thought I was better than everybody. I thought I was a more naturally gifted singer, so I didn't try. I didn't learn the parts I was supposed to. I floated through alto, tenor, soprano — whatever harmony I liked the most.

Instead of trying to become a better team player or improve my sight-reading skills, I spent all my time watching the older boys twirl around the girls my age. I mean literally pick up and toss around the girls my age. In a ritualistic pubescent display, the boys would pick up the girls and just run around. The girls, draped over their broad shoulders, would gleefully bang on their backs. They would yell things like, "Will! Put me down!" or "Oh my gosh, you're gonna drop me!" And the boys would be like, "Me big. Me big man. Me big man pick up small girl."

I never got picked up. I never got tossed around. I watched my friends fly through the air like carefree paper airplanes. I watched them giggle six feet off the ground, then land with a screech on the gym floor, their faces pink and their hair tousled. I watched them adjust their tiny hip-hugger jeans around their narrow hips, then go eat the doughnuts some parent brought in for break time. I watched them lick icing off their hands in the cafeteria while I clicked my fingers around my wrist under the table, just checking.

I left the choir when I was seventeen and got a job as the host of a national kids' show. I spent two days a week in an office writing episodes with my producer, then the other two days out in Manitoba somewhere, shooting. Like, "Hey guys! It's Hayley, and oh my gosh, you'll never guess where I'm standing right now. [Step back a bit; camera zooms out] Yup! I'm in a snakepit in Morden, Manitoba, and today we are gonna learn about slithery, slimy snakes!"

We shot episodes in the public pool, the zoo, the golf dome, the science centre. We went to gardening nurseries and made Halloween costumes and learned how to bake together and paint together and make believe together.

And yes, one time, I did run with the dogs in the local best-in-show competition. They set me up on all fours alongside a Great Dane. I looked into the camera, beyond the fourth wall, and spoke to you at home in your den: "I can beat this guy. I bet he's not even that fast." Then the whistle blew and the dog sprinted away from me, majestically leaping over hay bales as I scrambled to get at least halfway through the obstacle course by the time the dog had finished.

I shot the show for two and a half years. I started making real money for the first time and feeling like a boss for the first time, while handling the precarious opportunity the show offered me, the opportunity to see myself on camera every single day.

I started building the List. The List was not written down. It was an invisible and private collection of foods that I stamped as edible or inedible.

Fat of any kind — Obviously inedible
Bread — Totally inedible
Dessert — Are you fucking kidding me?
Dairy — Totally inedible
Dressing — No chance
—

Canned tuna — Edible
Frozen peas — Edible
Raw mushrooms — Edible
Mustard — Great
Salsa — Basically just a very soft salad
Rice cakes with cinnamon — Oh my gosh, treat time!

The List worked. I lost twenty pounds I absolutely could not afford to lose. My clothes started falling off of me, and on a regular basis people told me they were worried, which might as well have been patting me on the back and whispering, *It's working, baby. Keep at it.* I got into regular fights with my parents and started exercising obsessively. Then I would stand in front of the bathroom mirrors and see no change, no difference. I would see right past my emaciated frame and skeletal shoulders and stare into the eyes of the girl at choir who never got picked up.

I would see the twelve-year-old who was too tall and too thick and way bigger than Mauri, then quietly click my fingers around my wrist, just checking.

I quit the show to go to Europe with Diego when I was nineteen. I knew I wouldn't be able to do both the show and the trip, so I talked to the head of the network and left. I packed up my ravenous desire to be loved and my total unwillingness to nourish my body and jumped into my intoxicating new romance with my mysterious new man friend, completely certain he was the love of my life.

diego

paris sucked

I woke up after Diego on one of the two Bert-and-Ernie-style single beds in our tiny room in a shitty-Paris hostel.

I don't mean the hostel itself was shitty. I mean a hostel in shitty Paris.

I woke up to his empty bed and the sound of the shower running. As we had been digitally getting to know each other over the previous few months, he had told me several times how much he loved showering. Now, after two weeks of travelling together, I saw that his telling me this was a sort of genius distancing technique. Like, make the girl believe it's your favourite thing early on, so that later you can hide in the bathroom as much as you want. Lock the bathroom door, run the water, and read or write or masturbate or whatever.

I crawled to the end of my bed and slumped to the ground, sitting cross-legged on the floor in front of my giant backpacking-style knapsack. I'd removed the metal back supports from this backpack before leaving Canada so I could fit in more clothes and two five-pound free weights. Yes, I did that — because body dysmorphia sucks.

I pulled out my pack of birth control pills and popped Sunday into my mouth. Looking over my shoulder to make sure Diego wasn't about to walk out of the bathroom, I stuck my right hand down the front of my pants to see if I was still bleeding.

In preparation for losing my virginity to him a few weeks earlier, I had gone on the pill. I'd been certain our trip would be filled with scandalous, spontaneous acts of passion, and I wanted to be prepared. Unfortunately, my period was due at the same time as this big romantic trip to Europe, so I attempted to skip it by going right from one pack to the next, jumping over the sugar pills you take during shark week. The problem is you can't really skip a period when you are new to birth control. So, rather than successfully skipping my period, I gave myself this sort of dripping-faucet half period for twelve fucking days.

With my hand down the front of my pants and my head turned over my shoulder, staring at the bathroom door, I discovered, to my horror, the long, thin string of a tampon. Meaning I had forgotten that I had that tampon in me for roughly sixteen hours.

I realized this the moment I heard the shower turn off. Quickly pulling my hand out of my pants, I resumed casually rummaging through my bag.

Diego came out of the bathroom, dressed and ready for the day. He said, "What are you gonna do today?"

Most days this question killed me. Like, weren't we on this trip together?

I pieced together a sentence in response as he walked to the door. "Gonna go for a run and walk around."

He mustered every ounce of his morning strength and tossed me the semblance of a smile, then picked up his small black journal and walked out.

I counted to three, making sure he was down the hall, then ran into the bathroom as my panic boiled to the surface. I sat on the toilet and yanked out the tampon, remembering the tiny warnings on the back of every tampon box. Warnings that in my memory read something like this: *Toxic shock syndrome is what you get when you stupidly forget you have your period and leave a tampon in for sixteen hours and, yes, you have it, Hayley. And yes, you're gonna die from it. In shitty Paris. Alone. While he who will never love you is out fucking a gorgeous French painter with an adorable little bob and an impossibly fast metabolism.*

I threw on something beige and corduroy, grabbed my wallet, and left our room.

On my way out, I ran into one of the hostel employees, who said, "Oh, hey, listen. You need to pay for another night by one p.m. today if you're gonna stay. Otherwise we have to move your stuff out of the room." I nodded hard, trying to shake my tears back into my head.

We had been taking turns paying for the rooms, and it was his turn to pay. I guess in the interest of putting as much distance between us as quickly as possible, he had just motored past the front desk. The problem, however, was that it was the weekend and I was out of cash until I could get to a bank the following day.

So, it was 10:00 a.m., and I now had three hours to take myself to a hospital, figure out whether I was dying or not in a language

I barely understood, and somehow get a couple hundred bucks so we wouldn't get evicted, all while he napped under a tree somewhere in shitty Paris. In true me fashion, I chose not the issue that was maybe, possibly, most likely killing me, but the issue that would more immediately affect him. I walked up to a young woman and stumbled through a string of nonsensical bank-themed French.

Envisioning again the tampon-box warning label and list of symptoms, I calmed myself by remembering that throwing up was one of the most common symptoms of toxic shock. As long as I didn't barf, I was fine.

I ran toward the bank machine, dodging vendors in a busy fruit market and passing happy families and couples in love, all eating bread, all thin. As I weaved in and out of traffic, my stomach gurgled, and as my lips failed to stay clenched together, I barfed on the sidewalk.

I burst into tears and threw my hand in the air to hail a cab. A car pulled up in front of me almost immediately. I collapsed into the back seat and said "Hospital!" in a terrible French accent, as if that would help the driver understand me. I pushed my arms against my stomach and scanned the interior of his cab. A tiny, bouncing bobblehead of a character I didn't recognize was suctioned to the dashboard beside a small photograph of three beautiful children climbing on an exquisite woman. A blatant reminder of what I would never have, now that I was dying and all.

The driver turned around and passed me his card, saying, "When you are done, you call me, and I will take you home."

I regressed with a look that said, *Thank you. I'm scared. I want my mommy*, and pushed his card into my back pocket.

I walked into the hospital and up to a friendly looking receptionist. I took a deep breath and tried to get my story out without sobbing on her. "I. Think. Toxic. Shock."

Five minutes later, a nurse came out to grab me and lead me into a doctor's office. I sat on the little checkup bed, my legs dangling off the side, making me feel even more like a child. Being sick makes me feel very young. Desperate to have a parent rub my back and bring me saltines and ginger ale.

A doctor who spoke very little English walked in. He asked me to lay on my back. He pressed his fingers into my abdomen and then said, "No toxic shock."

Relieved that I was not going to die, and confused at how quickly he determined the diagnosis, I said "*Merci*" and left.

I sat on a stoop and pulled out my ten-dollar pay-as-you-go flip phone to call the cabby. He arrived a few minutes later, as promised. I told him I was, in fact, not going to die, which I was pleased about, then asked him to drop me at the bank machine by the hostel.

I was pretty sure it wouldn't work, but I was desperate and had to try. I put in my card, begging the machine to ejaculate money onto me. Which it refused to do.

As is usually my response to anything that goes wrong in my life, I called my dad. As I waited for him to pick up, I collapsed to the ground under the bank machine, a few feet away from a homeless dude, who looked over and gave me an understanding nod.

My magical father said, "Sit tight. Keep checking your account."

I leaned against the bank machine, checking my account every ten minutes for a full hour with no luck, inching closer to the reality of having to go back to the hostel, watch the staff dump our stuff onto the street, and tell Diego that it was all my fault.

I'm still not entirely sure how my dad did it, but somehow he reached down from the sky, waved his magic wand, and wired machine-accessible money to my account on a Sunday. I pulled out a few hundred bucks and ran back to the hostel with twenty minutes left before our stuff would be removed from our room.

I ran through the front door, past the tables of young travellers consulting spread-out maps, marking routes for day trips. I walked up to the counter, slapped my cash on the table, and said, "I'm paying for another night in room one twelve."

Now, finally able to breathe for the first time since I'd woken up, I decided to go for a walk. A walk to remind myself that Paris wasn't a horrible nightmarish shithole. I strolled around until I had sufficiently shifted the day's focus, then decided to go back to the hostel and use my final few hours of alone time to lie in bed and be unselfconscious. To nap and not worry about what I looked like or in what ways I was being judged or what decisions were being made about me without my knowledge. To just sit in my body and not hate myself for a few hours.

As I walked back to the hostel, people watching, city watching, I scanned the charming patio of a little restaurant. And there he was, Diego. Sitting peacefully at a small circular table with his journal open and an elegant coffee mug in his hand. He looked calm and settled and happy for the first time since I'd landed in Montreal. He looked like himself for the first time since I'd landed in Montreal.

He looked up and saw me standing a few feet away, then pressed some sort of bright-red panic button under the table, causing an invisible force field to shoot up around him in a perfect protective orb. With my self-consciousness back in full swing and his peaceful quiet time sufficiently ruined just by seeing me, I sat cautiously beside him.

"How was your day?" I asked.

"Nice. I just strolled. Did some writing. What did you get up to?"

"Not much. Just walked around. It's such a nice day."

diego

emotional amnesia

We had been following a fold-out map in Diego's Lonely Planet guide to Barcelona for what felt like a hundred years, trying dejectedly to find the hostel, peeking in and out of romantic back alleys, their romance having no effect on us. We could have stumbled upon a proposal flash mob dancing to Bruno Mars's "Marry You," and unless it was flash-mobbing us in the direction of the hostel entrance, we would have found it obnoxious and over the top, which of course every flash mob is.

By this point in the trip, I was just scared of Diego. I was scared to speak to him; I was scared to answer any questions; I was scared to sound stupid; I was scared to look at him; to eat and breathe and exhale. My insecurities and general feelings of inadequacy sat beside me like a gluttonous, unwanted dinner guest. Reaching over my plate, grabbing my favourite things right out of my hand, then pouring full glasses of red wine onto the rest of my food while laughing at me. Its dripping lips pressed tightly against my ear; its hot breath and sharp, grazing teeth reminding me who was in charge.

What I didn't know how to do at nineteen was turn and look my unwanted dinner guest directly in its fat pustule of a face and say, *I see you. Now get the fuck out of my house.*

We went around one more corner, onto a road I could have sworn we'd been down before, and there it was. Diego turned around to look at me, smiling and relieved. I took these milliseconds of softness as assurances that he was in fact deeply in love with me. I took these moments of warmth as indicators that I was crazy for thinking otherwise.

We walked up the winding staircase and checked in. He grabbed our key from the counter and guided us down the steadily narrowing hallway. Looking down to make sure the number on the key matched the number on the door, he stopped and let us into room 19. He flicked on the light with his left index finger, revealing, to my horror, a set of bright-red bunk beds.

I swallowed hard, trying not to cry, trying to will away my gluttonous, unwanted dinner guest, who was now soaring over me, standing on the dining table, pointing and laughing at my face, its razor-sharp nails digging into my plate as the last of my chocolate cake mushed out between its toes.

Defeated, I climbed up the metal ladder and placed my bag on the top bunk.

It was already late, so we started getting ready for bed almost immediately. Diego got out his little toiletry bag, the specific dimensions and identifying characteristics of which

I had now memorized. The blue fabric, the quarter inch of plastic surrounding the zipper, the faded dime-sized toothpaste stain from the bumpy train we took from Portugal to Italy. The bumpy ride that I thought would be fun and charming and a snapshot of *Before Sunrise*. A bumpy ride that ended up being nothing but bumpy.

He disappeared into the hallway, momentarily letting in a cacophony of languages as he opened the door. I lay on the top bunk waiting for him to return so I could go brush my teeth and get myself ready for yet another night of literally praying for a touch, a hug, a kiss, eye contact, anything.

When he came back into the room, he collapsed immediately onto his bottom bunk, leaving the door slightly open for me. His only real acknowledgement that I existed in the space at all.

I tiptoed down the ladder, careful not to move or breathe or express too much of anything with my body language. Deliberately robotic in the hopes of remaining palatable to him. I slipped into the hallway, quietly pulling the door shut behind me as if he were a sleeping baby.

Small gaggles of travellers joyfully pulsed through the hallway, laughing about their insane adventures. About the cabby who tried to rob them, the waiter that spilled beer all over that guy they met in Rome at that museum. The guy who then took them to that house party on that island where they roasted hot dogs in that millionaire's fireplace and met Leonardo DiCaprio. They spun around me, their limbs lovingly twisted around each other, these radiant symbols of the trip I'd desperately wanted to have.

I got to the bathroom, splashed some cool water on my face, brushed my teeth, and walked back down the hallway to room 19. I inched the door open, reaching out and quietly tracing the metal bed frame in the pitch blackness, leaving all the light and joy and connection in the hallway behind me.

Wishing I was weightless, I lay back on my bed, desperate to remain quiet, desperate to not disturb him. I stared up at the ceiling, my eyes slowly getting used to the darkness. Slowly able to make out the bits of water damage, the mysterious stains, the poorly painted-over signatures and messages of love written in dark-blue Sharpie.

In the midst of counting the number of hours we had left together before leaving the following morning, I heard him shift beneath me. I heard him shift out of his sheets, I heard him shimmy his legs off the side of the bed, I heard him stand, and I felt the bed rock as he touched my little red ladder. My heart pounding in my chest, I felt him slowly inch his way up onto my top bunk. He nudged his body over me in the silence and pulled my sheets to one side.

With my pulse in my lips, my ears, my fingers, I thought about pressing my hand against the back of his head, still watching the ceiling and the bits of water damage and the mysterious stains and the poorly painted-over signatures and messages of love all now shifting along with his exhalations. I yelled at my hand with my mind, trying to will it to participate but feeling like it was somehow inappropriate to touch him even though he was in my body.

He finished a few minutes later and nudged his body off me and inched his way down my little red ladder and back onto his bottom bunk. He may have mentioned something about the size of the top bunk being impractical for the purposes of sleeping two adult people, which of course it was. But I was nineteen. Practical sleeping conditions were not my top priority.

I lay on my back, so angry and so confused. So happy to have been touched at all and so confused as to why I felt so empty seconds later. So confused, fifty seconds after the act, to not even be able to access the feeling of it. So confused as to why I could not participate in ways I wished I could. To not be able to engage my lips and my ears and my fingers. To not be able to pull him into me, to wrap my hand around the back of his neck, to demand his mouth on mine.

I rolled onto my left, wedging a pillow between my legs and measuring the moments it took for his long, deep breaths to become low, rumbling snores.

I woke up on my back, now able to more clearly make out the water damage and not-so-mysterious stains and poorly painted-over signatures and messages of love. Rubbing my eyes, I flung my legs onto my little red ladder, tiptoeing down to find his bottom bunk empty except for his little blue toiletry bag, with its quarter inch of plastic surrounding the zipper and its faded dime-sized toothpaste stain.

I grabbed my overworked bright-red journal and decided to sit on the back patio until he appeared again. I opened our door and entered the stream of happy travellers making day plans in a number of languages, with their limbs joyfully draped around each other. I walked down the hall and out onto the gorgeous back patio, a small slice of the Barcelona sky overrun by plants and twinkly lights and wooden tables covered with chiselled-out hearts with initials inside.

Looking around for somewhere to sit, I found him, leaning against the building, writing in his journal. He looked up, made uninterested eye contact with me, then went right back to his writing. I felt like I had on my first day of grade seven, starting junior high, walking through a foreign cafeteria, desperate for a welcoming stranger to kick out a nearby chair and motion me and my stinky tuna sandwich over.

I pressed my bright-red journal to my chest, smiled like an apology, and walked past Diego to sit down at the corner table, under the large leaves of some majestic overhanging plant. I began writing: *I don't understand why I'm here. Why did he want to come on this trip with me? It's like I'm invisible. Am I that gross? Am I that unlovable? He can't even make eye contact with me?* I finished my heartfelt entry, then closed my bright-red, overworked journal. I pressed it back against my chest and walked back into our room without even attempting eye contact with him.

The wobbly ladder shook as I climbed back up on my bunk to begin collecting my things, shoving them into my sad, disappointed backpack. My two rectangular packages of birth control pills slipped out of a side pocket to mock me: *Oh yeah? Did you have a super fun, sexy time?*

I was about to push my journal into the front flap and zip it shut on this bullshit trip when he burst into the room. He rushed in like a different person. Like a friend, even. Like someone happy to see me.

"It's our last day in Europe. Let's get some food and walk around or something. I'm gonna go brush my teeth, then let's get out of here." He grabbed his little blue toiletry bag, and before he disappeared into the hall, he looked back at me, smiling.

The second the door shut behind him I pulled out my journal, drew a long, hard line through the middle of the page and started writing directly beneath my "WTF, am I invisible?" entry from five minutes earlier.

I wrote, *I'm so dumb. Disregard top of this page. Everything is fine. We're gonna go get some food now and walk around until we have to head to the train station. I'm so dumb. He was just tired.*

The great tragedy of my trip really happened on the way home, when I left my overworked, bright-red journal in the seat pocket on my last flight back to Winnipeg. I had been too busy sobbing in the bathroom, staring at myself in the mirror and lip-synching to Imogen Heap's "Hide and Seek" as it blared into my headphones to have the wherewithal to make sure I took all my belonging with me upon disembarking.

I went to the airport lost and found for weeks after but never got it back. Some fucker out there has my journal, which is devastating, as no other single page of journaling has ever said more about me.

tal

two thin red lines

It is an actual miracle that I never contracted any sort of sexually transmitted disease, because — as I was hyperaware — Tal was constantly fucking other women, sometimes several in a day, sometimes while I was in the next room.

It was July. The third July we'd spent together. We fucked over and over.

I woke up that morning in his bed. In a gorgeous tree house in the Hollywood Hills, cottagey and welcoming, though maybe I felt that way because I'd helped him pick it out after we'd looked at several other homes together. We had walked through properties all over the city. He asked if I liked the neighbourhood, the light, the potential for a studio in the back, seeking my approval as if the house were a gift for me.

I rolled over to grab my phone and responded to some text message. He leaned over to see who it was, and out of instinct I turned the screen away from him, though it was not a particularly devious message.

He said, "What? You don't have to hide shit from me, Hayley. Ain't nobody having a baby."

He went to the studio, but as I drove home to my new Tal-less apartment in Silver Lake, his words ran mysterious laps in my head. I thought it was such a strange thing to say, and it poked at me from the passenger's seat as I drove by pharmacy after pharmacy. It rested its muddy shoes on my dashboard and obnoxiously motioned to every Walgreens, Ralphs, Rite Aid. It tore open a bag of chips and wiped its oily hands on the seat as we approached the giant pastel-pink dollar store on Sunset. It leaned its wet mouth over to my ear and said, *We should probably stop here.*

I turned and acknowledged my chip-eating, crumb-leaving driving companion and parked. I walked inside to fill my basket with a bottle of coconut water, a kitchen sponge, cockroach repellent, and a pregnancy test. I tossed my four dollars on the counter without making eye contact with the cashier; shoved the long, cheap cardboard box in my pocket; and drove home, the test burning a hole in my thigh.

I sat on the toilet, ripped the packaging open with my teeth, and pulled out the tiny plastic wand. I curled over and shoved it under me, looking down to make sure I was peeing directly onto it. Then I lay it on the cold, grey linoleum between my feet.

With my panties around my ankles, I held my head in my hands as I watched the test come to life, magically, deliberately, confidently painting two hard red lines.

My mouth fell open as I took a hard, shallow breath from my throat and began quietly weeping. I'd always thought I might want kids. But not like this. Not with an unkind man who didn't love me, who had another relationship and constantly broke any semblance of trust between us.

I walked back to my bedroom, suddenly feeling so pregnant. Suddenly feeling like I could feel the baby in me. Like I could feel this tiny collection of bones and organs and hair taking shape against my abdomen.

I grabbed my keys and drove around the corner to Planned Parenthood.

I buzzed the front door and they let me into the tiny second-floor Hollywood waiting room filled with young, scared-looking women, nervous and fidgety, flipping through magazines and trying not to stare at each other. I signed in at the front and became one of them.

"Hayley Penner?"

I followed a white nurse's coat through an unmarked door, my hands around my body, feeling so small, feeling like a baby myself.

"How can we help you today, honey?" she said.

"I just took a pregnancy test and it came out positive, so I just want to make sure."

She passed me a small plastic cup and gave me directions to the washroom down the bright, blinding, windowless hallway. Sitting on the cold plastic toilet seat, I pushed the cup beneath me this time, then opened the tiny door beside the sink and placed the container on the platform for the nurse to pick up on the other side.

I returned to the room where the nurse was and waited.

"So, you are pregnant. You are seven weeks. Is the father in the picture? You have lots of options."

As I tried to speak through my simmering tears, she passed me a document outlining the abortion services they offered. I took the paper and left, saying I needed to speak to him before I made any decisions.

I drove home, in a pure and singularly focused daze, barely paying attention to traffic signs and street lights. I curled into the fetal position on my bed and pulled out my phone to text him. *Hi. Can you call me when you're done at the studio? We need to talk.* Send.

He responded, *No we don't, I'm busy.*

I responded, *Yes, we do. I'm pregnant.*

My phone rang.

"Yes, I'm sure. I took a test and went to Planned Parenthood. I'm sure."

He told me to come meet him at the studio. I flew over the 101 and pulled up in front of his shitty-looking studio connected to a parking lot in the armpit of North Hollywood. I parked my car, texted him, got out, and sat on the curb with my knees pressed against my chest.

He walked up to me and said, "Hi, honey. Let's go," the tiniest edge of panic and annoyance seeping through his attempt at compassion.

I climbed into the passenger seat of his car, abandoning mine at the studio. We drove back to his tree house in the hills, up his long, winding driveway. We parked and went for a walk.

As we passed the massive, gorgeous homes and award-winning gardens, he said, "So, listen, I will support you with whatever you wanna do, but you know I can't have a baby now. I know this is tough, but just because you're pregnant doesn't mean we're really together now. I'm still with Molly. Even if we were to end up together, it can't be now. I can't have a baby now."

I stopped and bent over, my hands on my hips, trying to catch my breath. I said, "I've spent more time with you over the last three years than she ever has."

He stopped beside me. "Hayley, I've spent the last three years with a lot of girls."

For the first time in our relationship, I yelled, "Fuck you!" I started walking back toward his house, barely registering the scattered Franklin Canyon hikers peering into our conversation, trying to figure out whether we were famous or not.

I walked into the house ahead of him and went straight to his bedroom. I collapsed onto his bed and pulled a long pillow against my stomach.

Realizing the tough-love approach wasn't going to work, he curled up behind me and whispered in my ear. "Is this really what you want? You really want *my* baby? Now?" As I sobbed quietly, pressed against him, he whispered, "I'll pay for whatever you need. I'll send you home — you can be with your family, have it done in Canada. Whatever you want."

I sent him dates.

He sent me tickets.

I arrived in Toronto a few days later, picked up at the airport by my godmother. I spent the night at her beautiful home in a Rosedale high-rise. Brutally nauseous and unable to stomach anything. Water tasted acidic; fruit tasted rotten.

She sat on the couch and patted her lap, motioning me over. Exhausted, I laid my head against her thigh, her hands combing through my hair, my hand on my belly, knowing this was the first and only night the three of us would be cuddled together on that mustard-yellow couch.

I somehow managed to sleep both not well and for an uninterrupted ten hours. In the morning she quietly knocked on the door, eased it open, and crawled into bed with me.

Later, throwing a baby-blue trench coat over my sweatpants and T-shirt, I took a long look at myself in the mirror by the front door. Then, feeling her hand on my back, I stepped out into the hallway.

I leaned my head against the car window, watching the trees blur together into one thick, green wash. We walked up the staircase and entered the waiting room. Soft seats, natural light, and a handful of women reading articles in *Vogue* and *Cosmo*. "10 Ways to Know If He Likes You."

I went up to the counter, filled out my paperwork, and took the clipboard back to sit beside my godmother.

"Hayley Penner."

I followed a white nurse's coat into the next waiting room, a slightly upgraded space, like a change room in a spa.

"Is it going to hurt?" I asked.

She assured me it wouldn't, then passed me a hospital gown. She told me I might be a bit nauseated after, that it was normal, and that she would be waiting for me in recovery after it was over.

When she'd left the room, I slowly pulled off my clothes. Folding them into a little wooden cubby, I wondered how many other girls had piled their things in the same tiny space knowing they would be returning to get their stuff just a little bit emptier.

I walked down a short, dark hallway toward a tiny operating room. A doctor and three nurses already waiting for me as I walked in. They helped me up onto the table and guided my legs into the stirrups. A vintage-looking grey computer screen clicked on above me as they squeezed jelly onto an ultrasound wand and rubbed it against my abdomen.

I turned to look at the image, this tiny blue-grey flickering blur. With tears running down my cheeks, I looked up at the doctor.

"Are you sure you want to do this?" she asked.

I nodded my head yes.

She asked again. "Hayley, I need to hear your words. Is this a decision you and you alone have made, and are you sure you want to do this today?"

Crying, with my head bouncing between *yes* nods and *no* shakes, like a bobblehead on a dashboard, I squeezed out, "Yes, I am sure."

She put her hand on my shoulder. "Okay. This will take just a few minutes and will not hurt."

They gave me some sort of fast-acting anesthetic, and I dozed off as the doctor lifted my gown and disappeared between my legs.

A few minutes later, they helped me get up and off the table and escorted me to the recovery room. A room of pedicure massage chairs, with half-conscious girls sitting in a semicircle. A few throwing up into tiny trash cans, a few eating saltines off of paper plates, a few drinking orange juice, and a few just staring vacantly out the windows.

"Do you want cookies or crackers?" the floating white nurse's coat asked.

Thinking, *If ever there was a moment to quiet the voice in my head constantly calling me fat and just eat the fucking cookie, it's now*, I took two bites. Then I dropped my paper plate and threw up in the tiny trash can beside my chair.

I flew back to L.A. a week later. Tal called me as the plane landed, knowing the exact time of my arrival because he'd booked the flight. He asked me to come over.

I agreed, wanting so desperately to normalize the situation.

I arrived at his place to find his parents, his cousin, his cousin's wife, and their four-year-old daughter, Lena, visiting from Vancouver. I'd met them before. Lena spotted me at the door and leapt into my arms. His cousin looked at me, not knowing the two weeks I'd just had, and said, "If you guys had a baby, she'd look just like Lena."

I almost threw up.

I almost stabbed him.

I almost collapsed.

But instead I smiled, kissed Lena on the cheek, and lovingly put her down.

It took only a couple days for Tal and me to slip back into the same routine. Feeling like a shell of myself and committing what my psychoanalyst calls "psychic suicide," I pushed my brain off a high-rise at sunset and let my vacant body follow his.

Three months later he went to Canada to visit Molly. A month after that he told me she was pregnant and that they were having the baby and that she was going to move to L.A. so they could start their family.

She gave birth to a healthy, beautiful baby boy, completely oblivious to the events that would have made her new, healthy child an impossibility.

And now there is this gorgeous boy that feels like mine but isn't.

His existence is the result of a single decision I made.

I don't know him and will never know him, but I feel invisibly and irreversibly connected to him by two confident, hard red lines.

daniel

the standard hotel-room 911

One of the pleasures of being a late bloomer with low self-esteem is the willingness to try anything with anyone, anytime. So terrified that every first shot will be the only shot, we dive in headfirst to whatever is presented to us.

And we dive in even harder and faster when we are trying to forget about our recent abortion.

"You wanna hog-tie me till I pass out?" Sure, why not?

"You wanna roll me up in a carpet in an abandoned house?" Sounds cool.

"You wanna fuck in the back of this movie theatre?" Of course. Let me put the popcorn on the floor.

One of the pleasures of living in L.A. is the pool of celebrities you find yourself in. Rich, notable men who are more than interested in taking a break from their supermodels and actresses. Perhaps to remind themselves how far they've come or just to flex and dazzle a passably beautiful commoner.

I am a perfect subject for such men, and such men are the perfect subjects for me. Growing up with a famous father and being surrounded by fame all my life gave me a unique sense of normalcy around the whole celebrity thing. I can both be dazzled and feel totally at home while simultaneously recognizing that they are just men. Just dudes groping in the dark, like everyone else. Men who cry and shit and shower. Men who fuck up relationships and don't call their mothers enough.

I met Daniel on a hilarious celebrity dating app. It's possible it's like Fight Club and even mentioning it here will get me kicked off.

He was staying at the Standard downtown. I waited in the lobby in my black I'm-sure-to-get-fucked-in-this jumper, a leather jacket, and a new MAC lipstick shade called Vendetta. The elevator dinged and he came limping around the corner, wearing a boot from a recent injury. Like a big, sexy bear with a broken leg, just busted up enough to make me feel incrementally less intimidated.

I immediately made a joke about the boot.

A joke he missed.

A joke I had to awkwardly explain.

Something like, "I love your style. That boot is so edgy."

We crossed the street and sat down at a hip little restaurant. He ate chicken. I ordered some sort of rice vegetable situation. He does not drink. So I did not drink.

Then he sealed the deal by doing the things that always seal the deal. He made me laugh and he made me talk about myself.

He asked me questions about my family, then used my siblings' names in follow-up questions. He gave insights into my parents' divorce, into my dad's new marriage, into my shitty five-year affair with Tal. And he did it all with relentless eye contact.

So when the check came and he casually tossed his metal credit card on the table and said, "What do you want to do now, Hayley?" I smirked, started chewing on my thumbnail, and said, "I mean, you know what I want to do."

"You wanna come to my room?"

I bit my lip, nodded my head, and said, "Yes."

I stood silently in the elevator. Looking away, pretending not to feel his eyes on me, letting him scan my body without interference.

The door opened and he led me to room 911. "You're about to change my entire relationship to these numbers, aren't you?" I said.

This time, he laughed.

I walked in ahead of him and sat on the couch, looking back with the slightest edge of nervousness to assure him he was in charge. He sat beside me. Like an invitation, I draped my legs over his lap, just barely running my foot up his inner thigh.

Let's pretend I am the slightest bit modest and not get fully into who did what to whom. Let's just say the following things happened:

We watched 1970s porn at 3:00 a.m.

I wrote him a jingle for his character on a show I absolutely cannot name.

He surprise-slapped me across the face when I started cumming.

And at one point I thought he was going to bite my ear off — like, clean off.

But my favourite moment of the night, besides the alluded-to adult activities, happened at 4:00 a.m. Half-asleep, fully naked, partially covered, he gently released me from his grasp and stood up.

Like you'd do if you heard a large, mysterious animal outside your tent on a camping trip, I kept my eyes closed, careful not to expose my consciousness. Squinting one eye open, I watched his beautiful, lumpy, vulnerable, out-of-shape body trace the wall in the darkness. Clumsily avoiding a totally unnecessary number of iPhone chargers and empty sparkling-water bottles.

He reached down and pulled out a small box, then began picking at it. Like opening a candy wrapper in a silent movie theatre, he moved very quickly, then very slowly, then very quickly again.

Finally, releasing the packaging onto the floor,

he stood,

naked in a fancy hotel room,

in the middle of the night,

on a one-night stand,

and ate an entire box of Oreos.

And I thought, *Fuck, I'm in love.*

We woke up in the morning and adult-activitied one more time before he had to get ready for his ride to the airport. I stood on the bed like a queen looking down on her achievements, my hands in my hair, delicately daring him to pack me in his carry-on.

On our way out of the room, he passed me a leather swag bag from the Emmys, which included the following things:

1.　a sheepskin blanket,
2.　an Amazon subscription,
3.　marble coasters,
4.　hand-carved wooden bowls, and
5.　a loose pair of Oliver Peoples glasses — which he definitely didn't mean to give me.

We walked to the waiting car. He wrapped his giant arms around me, kissed me, and said, "I'd like to see you again." I watched him drive away.

About an hour later he sent me a screenshot of one of my songs on Spotify, fangirling in a way that definitely meant he'd assumed I was shitty. I responded with a picture of his handprint on my ass and a voice note of me singing the jingle I wrote for his character on the show I absolutely cannot name.

daniel

the east village

I woke up in Daniel's tiny East Village apartment the morning of my last day in New York. I woke up the way I had the previous three mornings, cuddled against his warm barrel chest under the painting of a prairie sky on fire, a painting he'd spent fourteen thousand dollars on, a painting he'd purchased with his ex.

I quietly pulled the sheets off and dressed in one of his T-shirts and a pair of white panties. I tiptoed over to stand in front of his overflowing wall of books and grabbed one. I thought he might find it sexy to see me pretending to read, curled up on the couch.

I waited for him to stir so I could quickly toss on my fake glasses, mess my hair, rest *War and Peace* on my chest, and look up at him as if to say, *Oh, I didn't realize you were up.*

As I listened to him breathe, I put my legs up on the armrest and began memorizing the room, taking it in the way you do when you know you probably aren't going to see something again, romanticizing every corner of his messy, tiny apartment. The tobacco scattered on the coffee table, the stacks of empty to-go cups, the step-by-step "How to Eat a Woman Out" guide thumbtacked to the wall, the razor-sharp tip of a screw poking through the back of his open closet (the result of his being too lazy to go back to the hardware store for a shallower screw), and the photo on his windowsill. The photo of him with a group of actors, Meryl Streep included, Kevin Kline included, Christopher Walken included ...

It was Sunday morning. I had flown to New York the previous Thursday. A flight I wouldn't let him pay for. Like, "Yeah, that's right, I'm a self-sufficient, independent woman. Look at me showcasing my self-sufficient independence for the sole, specific, deliberate purpose of hopefully making myself more desirable to you."

I arrived to find him standing with a bouquet of flowers in an apartment full of candles. We spent three beautiful days together. Fucking and talking and crying and walking. He made plans for us all over the city. We slid to the front of every line at every restaurant as I overheard "Oh my god, that was ..." We watched an old western in a rundown East Village theatre, one of his hands on my thigh while the other shoved movie-theatre banana bread into his mouth, and two of the six other movie-goers got into a fight about midmovie cellphone use. I walked beside him on the filthy New York City streets as he told me about his life and his exes, showing me specific places where he did specific things.

I ran my fingers through his hair on the grimy, romantic subway while I watched the faces of the men and women and children around us who were trying to hide their excitement. They would whisper and point to each other; parents would kneel beside their children and motion, grinning, at our little impenetrable bubble, quietly recognizing my proximity-based specialness.

Daniel always noticed, though he would often pretend not to. He would pull his hat down over his forehead to avoid the paparazzi while I smiled politely on his behalf at the vibrating audience around us. I would nod my head and knowingly smile like the *Mona Lisa*, giving them a silent *Yes, it is him and, yes, he's fucking me.*

We stayed in. I made risotto with roasted chicken, a go-to date-night meal I make for men when I am trying to make them fall in love with me. I cook like a sweet and lovely little housewife, then I clear the table and help them digest with my head between their legs while they're still seated at the dining room table. Like, "Look no further. I can provide you with everything you need forever and ever, amen." Like, "Stop looking. Pick me." Totally certain that my value is exclusively connected to the services I provide.

He showed me a two-hour documentary on this dude who created a video game called *Meat Boy*. A small, square-shaped character with no skin — just a chunk of meat even the softest of corners could injure. Now I lay on his couch feeling like Meat Boy, tender and exposed, counting down our final few hours together.

He woke up with a groan, gutturally croaking my name into the room: "Haaayley." I smiled and said his name back in the same way: "Daaaniel." Laying the book on my chest, I waited for him to sit up and find me on the other side of the built-in shelf dividing the sleeping area from the rest of the bachelor apartment.

He hobbled over to me, looking exhausted, still recovering from his injury. He lifted my legs, sat on the couch, and draped them over his lap. Running his hands up my thighs, he looked over to his guitar in the corner and said, "So, you gonna finally sing something for me or what?" I smiled shyly, then stood up to get the guitar. Over the few weeks between the Standard and the East Village, he'd asked me a number of times to send him singing voice notes of his favourite songs, so I knew singing for him in person would only help my get-him-to-love-me campaign.

He began rolling his hundredth cigarette of the weekend as I sat back down on the couch with the guitar, quickly debating what to play. I settled on one of my own songs, "Sleep at Night," a song about telling Molly everything that had happened with Tal — hypothetically telling her. I sang it perfectly, feeling my face morph through every shade of pink.

I finished and looked up at him. He frowned, took a long pause, and said, "Yeah, you're not good." Then he smiled, leaned over, and kissed me. "Mind if we take care of some business before we stroll around today?"

"Yeah, of course," I said, having no idea what he meant.

We fucked and showered and dressed and left, grabbing a quick coffee from his favourite café on the way. I walked with a deliberately increased amount of space between us, trying to fool him into thinking I wasn't needy or desperate for physical contact. We strolled through his neighbourhood as I imagined where he might be taking me.

Maybe he'd made a reservation for us in some trendy Greenwich Village restaurant.

Maybe he'd bought me that two-thousand-dollar guitar he'd made me serenade him with at that music store we stumbled into during our last walk.

Maybe he's taking me to some seemingly ordinary corner where, he'll tell me, his twin brother had been struck by a speeding taxi and died when they were six. And I'll spontaneously step up onto a lonely milk crate and press his wet face against my chest, and I'll hold his bearded cheeks in my hands and kiss his salty lips and tell him there was nothing he could have done.

I looked up to find him motioning to a giant Rite Aid.

We passed the rows of makeup, the tampons, the condoms, the lube, making our way to the pharmacy counter at the back. He pulled his black baseball hat down over his Neanderthal fore-head as we approached a tiny pharmacist. I let him go up to the counter on his own, pretending to be enamoured by the selection of hair elastics and blow-dryers.

He returned to me a few minutes later with a familiar plastic box and a full Dixie cup. "Hope you don't mind. Just to be safe, you know?"

We inched into the corner by the clearance rack. I ripped open the box with my teeth to reveal the perfect blue morning-after pill in its perfect airlocked little home. I popped it out and put it in my mouth.

He passed me the water and I handed him the empty box. Shooting the pill back, I looked up at him, soaring over me. I clasped my hands behind my back and stuck out my tongue, lifting it up and side to side, proving to him that I had swallowed it.

He laughed and said, "Asshole."

daniel

pinky swears

We had an hour before I had to head to the airport. I forced myself to walk a foot away from Daniel because I couldn't do what I actually wanted to do. I wanted to jump up into his lumpy body, rest my head on his shoulder, and wrap my legs around his waist like a monkey. I wanted him to be it. I wanted him to be the answer. I wanted him to save me from myself. I wanted to be done.

He led me through a park. I'm sure *When Harry Met Sally* was shot there.

We'd walked out of the Rite Aid a few minutes before, joining the scattered New Yorkers in scarves and Blundstones, who
refused to look either way while crossing the street. I had just
taken the morning-after pill and it was already making me emotional. I was already feeling small and raw like Meat Boy when
Daniel said, "Not that it would be the worst thing for you to have
my baby. You're gonna be a great mom one day."

I forced a smile like I was lifting impossibly heavy weights
with the corners of my mouth. Trying desperately not to cry.
Trying desperately not to let the sagging pout pull my face down
the way it does when I start tearing up. Pretending to be distracted by the soaring skyscrapers in the hopes that he would not
notice my face becoming one giant red splotch, my eyes a crisp,
shattered, devastated, frozen blue.

We found a bench in the middle of the lush park, its furry
wildlife replaced by families and love. Men in love with women.
Women in love with women. Men in love with men. Children in
love with dogs and plants and abandoned trash. It was a perfect
New York autumn day, and all I wanted to do was rest my head
on his shoulder and I couldn't even do that. Locked inside myself,
too afraid I'd reveal that I, in fact, have needs.

Two friends of his walked by. He told them how we'd met on
the celebrity dating app I cannot name. They started talking about
Daniel's social media and how he always looks so serious. With a
totally straight face, I said that his publicist told him smiling ruins
his image and he's contractually obligated to always look angry.

They said, "What? Really?"

I said, "No. Not really."

Everyone laughed and I thought, *Oh, he's definitely gonna
love me now.* I fully thought that single joke might buy us an
entire relationship, or at least a chance at one. I felt proud of
myself. Like I'd just given him a peek into how funny and quick
and awesome I am. Like I was a car showing off my brand-new

leather seat covers. Like, "Look how comfy I can be. Look how relaxed your friends are with me. Look how seamlessly you could ride me to family dinners and friend's engagement parties and nieces' birthday parties. Look, I fit."

He was hungry. I was, too, but also, I didn't want a lobster sandwich, which is what he wanted. We started walking back through the neighbourhood toward his place, and I started counting, counting in my head.

Counting my steps.

Counting the blocks to his house.

The words exchanged between us.

The number of times we'd fucked.

The minutes left.

The miles between L.A. and New York.

I sat outside on a curb, waiting for him as he popped into the little lobster-sandwich place to get his food. The counting of significant Daniel-related things quickly developed into the counting of Daniel-adjacent things. Counting the number of couples on the street, how many of the women I deemed more beautiful than me. The number of men who would never be interested in me. The number of billboards I'd have to see his face on in a few months.

We walked the final block to his place. He smelled like lobster, even though his sandwich remained tightly bundled in its little tinfoil sleeping bag.

His building was surprisingly rundown for someone as famous as he was. I think it's because he was brand new to his particular level of fame. I stood in his tiny elevator, knowing that even if we were together for a long time, this would probably be the last time I saw this building.

I measured how close he was to me.

Waiting for the door to open in three … two … one …

Counting again.

He led me again, for the last time, down his long hallway. His unit was situated exactly where his Standard hotel room was. It might as well have been room 911, tucked in the corner. I wanted to say something funny, something to jolt his memory back to that first night.

I had eleven minutes before I had to call my Uber. Counting again.

He left his coat on and walked to the corner of his apartment. He sat down and opened the tinfoil sleeping bag onto his messy desk, beside the window it would have been easy to dive out of. He motioned for me to come over to him, moaning with a mouth full of lobster and white bread and mayo. He pushed his face into my stomach while he chewed. His jaw opening and closing against my soft, imperfect tummy.

He looked up at me and extended his pinky. "Promise me you'll always tell me how you feel. Promise me you won't hide things from me."

I started crying. Already so full of unsaid things. The weights attached to the corners of my mouth pulling my cheeks down.

I interlocked my pinky with his. I bet doing something this juvenile made him feel old and far away from a time when this was a totally binding form of agreement. It made me feel young. It does not feel so long ago that looping pinkies was as significant as slicing the tips of our fingers and pushing our bloody prints together.

I said, "Just don't lie to me. And please don't disappear."

He wrapped his greasy left hand around the back of my neck and pulled me in for a kiss. My forehead against his.

"So, I'm gonna come see you in Toronto next week. Then maybe you come visit me when I'm shooting down south?" he said.

"Yes. I would really like that," I said.

"Really? You really want me to come?"

"Yes, Daniel. Of course I do."

We were stuck in this moment. Me, floating on my good fortune. Hovering over myself, still unable to fully grasp that this big, important man was touching me. That this big, important man was insecure and desperate for my reassurance.

In the same moment he said, "Shouldn't you call your Uber?"

"Fuck. Yeah."

I ordered one and it arrived almost immediately. He kissed me one more time, then hugged me while remaining seated.

He didn't get up.

He didn't walk me to the door.

I listened to him chewing as I rolled my carry-on through his tiny apartment. I turned around to say goodbye and watched him take the last bite of his lobster sandwich.

I whispered, "See you next week."

Then never saw him again.

ben ⌇ cye ⌇ diego ⌇ daniel

desperate tactics

Daniel started drifting like a beach ball on a wave in the ocean, just barely out of reach. No matter how hard I swam and strategized and sent graphic, homemade pornographic content, something had shifted. Something he refused to share with me. Something he held quietly to his chest from the other side of the country.

He started disappearing just after I got back to L.A. from New York and just after he had bought me a ticket to come visit him. I tried to relax into the increasing space between my little blue text bubbles. I tried to understand and say, "He's busy. It's fine. Everything's fine."

He eventually asked me to pay to change the ticket, moving the trip back a week. Then he disappeared again, resurfacing two days before my flight to tell me not to come.

I did not handle this well. At first, I was all cool and strong and, "Well shit, if that's how you feel. I deserve better ... blah blah blah."

This was followed by the let's-be-friends approach. Nine out of ten men see right through this and remain quiet.

I shifted from this offer of friendship into deep, bubbling rage. I handwrote him a five-page letter detailing his shitty behaviour in essay form, then typed it up and printed it from a do-it-yourself kiosk at Kinko's before mailing it to his home address.

With Ben, my response to dump town was even more desperate and even less creative. I gently filled his inbox with photos of us together and in love. Photos of him pressed against my naked body, photos of his family, photos of our trip to Hawaii. Hoping to spark some sort of "Oh shit, I forgot, I *am* still in love with her!" reaction.

I showed up at his house a couple of times. Tried to kiss him a couple of times, tried to fuck him a bunch of times. It was a laser show of desperately bad choices.

My most impressive and embarrassing refusal to handle the reality of a loss was with Diego. When our Paris trip ended and I'd returned to Winnipeg, I spent weeks writing him letters, calling, emailing. I tried everything I could imagine to get him to engage with me. Like, *There must be something I haven't tried yet. There has to be some combination of things that will revive his feelings for me.*

I was ill-equipped to handle such immersive time together followed by such silence. One night, walking home, I blacked out on my block. I woke up on the ground a few minutes later, wondering how I had gotten there. When I got home, I avoided talking with my family and went directly to my little third-floor suite.

My private phone line rang. I looked at the caller display and saw Diego's name. I felt a sort of punch in the chest, like the time I grabbed on to the beam going into the basement, overswung, and landed directly on my back, knocking all the air out of me in one hard thump.

I picked up the phone and tried my very best to sound casual and fine. "Oh, hey, how are you? … Hello?"

I leaned back onto the big forest-green beanbag pillow in the corner of my room and tried to make out the faint speaking and moving and clanking of things coming from the other end.

He had pocket-dialed me.

It took me a few minutes to realize what had happened. I pushed the receiver into my face and silently wept. Unable to put it down, unable to let go of the closeness, unable to snip the tether he had accidently anchored me to. I curled up in the fetal position and balanced the phone on the side of my head, covering my soaked face with both hands, muting my gasps of pain with a palm over my mouth.

I lay with the phone against my chest and listened to his muddled movements and laughter and Spanish. I spent fifteen minutes like this. Fifteen full, excruciating minutes.

Somewhere just after fifteen, I panicked and thought, *Fuck, what if he does pick up at this point and then realizes I've been waiting for him to speak this whole time.* I thrust the receiver onto its hard little receiver bed and finished up my cry alone.

A couple weeks later, I planned a trip to San Francisco, knowing he'd be there. I planned it in the hopes of seeing him, bumping into him at the very least. I messaged him, all casual and shit: *Oh hey, as luck would have it, I'm gonna be in San Francisco exactly when you are! What are the chances?!* He never responded.

I spent three days pacing up and down Haight Street looking for him. I walked by cafés and clothing stores, peering past my floundering reflection in the hopes of seeing his shape buying a shirt at a counter or sipping a coffee while scribbling in his journal.

With Cye, I messaged his mom for a couple weeks after he broke up with me. Strategizing with her as to how to get him to continue loving me. She filled my inbox with emails begging me not to give up on her son. I sent her emails back telling her I wouldn't.

I would like to think my ability to handle loss has matured as I've gotten a bit older. That my reactions have become more sophisticated and refined. I would like to think that's the case, but it's not. My body holds on to pain only while I'm in it. The second the pain ends, so does my body's memory of it. It gets up and walks out of the room. It tosses me a peace sign over its shoulder, then closes the door behind it like it was never there at all. It entirely disarms my heart again, encouraging me to lay it at my next conquest's feet, raw and bloody, accompanied by a butcher knife, like a perfectly seared steak.

otis

red wine on a white rug

As instructed, Otis arrived promptly at 9:00 p.m. He walked through the entrance to my bedroom in that shared Silver Lake apartment with a bottle of wine in one hand and a motorcycle helmet in the other. He sat on the floor in front of my fireplace while I grabbed two glasses.

I pretended I didn't realize how aggressively short my shorts were and slowly sat next to him on the carpet. I pressed my elbow into the couch cushion and rested my cheek on my knuckles, deliberately leaving my pinky loose so I could periodically dip it into my mouth, forcing him to imagine other things inching toward my throat.

We finished the bottle of wine as he told me about recently relocating to L.A. from New York, a move he was finding challenging. I slipped my hand around the nape of his neck and promised him it would get better. I moved my fingers up into his thick black hair, inviting him into my own challenging story of moving to L.A., making sure to take long breaks from eye contact so he could watch my lips move, objectifying me the way I like.

I looked back at him, now inches from my face. I leaned in, almost touching his lips, then tilted my head back, making him reach for my kiss.

We quickly shifted over to the bed, sloppily pulling each other's clothes off. He kissed my lips and my neck, moving down my chest, making his way to my imperfect tummy, the birthmark on my hip, my thighs ...

I inhaled, deeply, audibly, preparing for ecstasy, my arms above my head, securing the pillow in my hands should I need to muffle my own voice. Then he started ...

Like trying to get a red-wine stain out of an expensive white carpet, he rubbed and rubbed and rubbed.

In excruciating pain, I pulled the pillow to my face and bit down hard, as if a doctor were attempting to pop a dislocated bone back into place. I let him go at it for what must have been just a few minutes, a few minutes that felt like a life sentence.

I reached down to give him a loving tap, benching him for the remainder of the game. He took the tap as encouragement and sped up his pace, rubbing harder and faster and deeper.

I could hear my vagina screaming, "What did I do to deserve this? Haven't I been good to you?"

Unable to take anymore, I opened a condom with my teeth and pulled him up against me.

He pushed his face into the pillow beside my head and jack-hammered for a few minutes, at which point his entire body tensed, he became several degrees hotter in an instant, made a noise like a goat, came, and collapsed on me. I rested my hand on the back of his head and gave him a respectful, slow, silent count to three before moving him off. He gave me the customary few final body spasms, then reached down to make sure the condom came out with him.

I stood up, grabbed the robe from my bedpost, and walked to the bathroom. The moment I was out of his line of vision, I clutched my traumatized vagina.

I delicately sat on the toilet. In response to the searing pain, I grabbed my thighs with both hands. Something was terribly wrong. I started examining the premises. Everything looked fine until I made eye contact with my clit, bright red and terrified like a little orphan jelly bean pleading, "Please don't hit me again." I reached down and realized ...

He had been rubbing so hard that he had slit it open, nearly disconnecting it from its adorable little hood altogether. I quietly panicked, then pressed a warm washcloth against it, staring at myself in the mirror, my panties around my ankles.

I tiptoed back into the room, not wanting to wake my clit now that she had finally fallen asleep. I got into bed and cuddled up to him, relying fully on the fact that the closer I cuddled, the less he'd want to have sex again.

We woke up early the next morning. He kissed me, grabbed his motorcycle helmet, and headed home to get ready for his serving shift at the restaurant he hated.

I listened to his motorcycle obnoxiously speed down my street, then tiptoed into the kitchen to grab an ice pack.

tal

you're not special

"Did Tal ever try anything with you?"

Melissa shifted in her seat, then said, "Yeah. Once."

In an instant she became the most important person in my life. Everyone else disappeared. I had no parents, no siblings, no friends, no casual dates with bad-in-bed guys — just her, her story, and me.

Melissa was a young woman, just like me, a woman who stepped wholeheartedly into Tal's camp with a flood of ambition and endurance. She ran errands and made coffee and untangled microphone cables in the hopes that she would one day be called into the studio and gifted the opportunity to prove herself as a skilled songwriter and musician. We all lived for these moments. We held on for these seemingly charitable gifts from on high. We waited and sacrificed our friendships and time and sense of self-worth for a sliver of an opportunity to touch beyond the velvet rope.

She leaned down and tied her tiny, hideous dog to the chair beside me on the patio of Republic of Pie. She said, "One sec, just let me go grab a coffee. I'm so glad I ran into you."

The dog and I stared at each other, mutually annoyed by each other's existence.

She came back and took the spot beside me, laying out a gluten-free poppyseed muffin on the table for us to share. Trying not to give away how desperate I was for every tiny fucking detail, I casually leaned in and said, "So, what happened?"

She launched in as if we'd planned to meet. "It was last year. They were performing in Toronto. I was back home visiting my family and he knew, so he asked if I could come, like, take pictures of them onstage and help out or whatever. So I went."

I picked at the muffin, unable to eat. She went on.

"The show was fine. I took pictures, then we went to this bar and he was drinking, which I thought was weird 'cause he, like, never drinks. And he was, like, buying me shots and shit. Then we were leaving and everyone was splitting up to go to their rooms and he just, like, slipped his arm under mine and said, 'She's gonna come with me' and nobody questioned it at all."

She paused to reach into her purse and lovingly serve a tiny brown turd of a treat to her ugly little dog. "He put on his gym clothes, then asked me to take pictures of him working out in the hotel gym, which was weird, but I did it. Then, like, thirty minutes later we went back to his room. He went into the bathroom and came out in a towel. Like, just a towel."

At this point in her story, my entire body was throbbing, heavy pulsing like I had shrunk down and climbed completely into one of those pharmacy blood-pressure-checking arm tubes.

She continued. "Sitting on the bed I was like, 'Oh, okay, I'll let you do your thing.' He walked over to me, sat down, and started kissing my neck, like, trying to take my shirt off. Then he put my hand on his dick.

"And I'm saying no and almost laughing a bit and pulling my shirt down and he just wouldn't stop, really, so eventually I, like, physically removed his hands from my body. Just got up and left. That was it."

It's easy to remain the other woman in an affair. You convince yourself you're special — in fact, you are so special that even though he has a gorgeous woman who loves him, he still needs *you*. Even though he is risking his professional reputation, it's worth it for *you*. It effortlessly feeds every insecurity you might have.

But finding out all of this about this girl, this girl who was no different than me — pulled into the same camp, hired to be around him — made me realize just how unspecial I was to him. It made me realize it had nothing to do with me. It was a sequence of events that any girl in my position could have gone through. It was not about my specific and unique characteristics. It was not about my heart or body or face, even. It was about my nearness. It was a matter of proximity and circumstance.

Seeing that I was panicking, she said, "Fuck, maybe I shouldn't have told you?"

I assured her she'd done the right thing by telling me, but told her I had to go. I walked to my car. Hyperventilating. As if a baby on the way wasn't enough.

I pulled out my phone and texted him. *I just ran into Melissa. She told me about what happened. Never talk to me again.*

My phone rang.

"Hey, sorry, what the fuck? What are you talking about? Nothing ever happened with her. She's crazy."

I hung up.

I began driving to the gym, feeling like a boiling kettle needing to blow off five years of steam. I walked quickly past reception, swiping my membership card with my glasses on so nobody would try to talk to my red splotchy face. I leaned my phone against my locker and slowly peeled my clothes off, my skin tender like I had the flu. I was pulling on my gym shorts when my phone lit up.

Melissa was calling.

"Hey, holy fuck, Hayley. So, I guess right after you talked to Tal, he called me. And I just had this feeling it was going to be fucked-up, so I waited until I got home to call him back ... waited till I got home so I could record the conversation."

Staring into the changing room mirror, shaking my head compulsively, I said, "I have to hear it. I'm sorry. I have to. Can I come over right now?"

She met me at the door of her tiny, messy apartment, holding her ugly dog, then escorted me in to sit in front of her computer. "This is fucked, Hayley, and probably hard to listen to. It's a lot. I don't even know if I should play it for you."

Not at all registering her warning, I leaned in, pressed the space bar, then placed my hands on my head.

The phone rang in the gurgled recording, then he picked up. His warbled voice played into her collapsing living room. He launched into one of his forty-five-minute monologues. After threatening her job and warning her that she didn't want to fuck with him, he picked up my lifeless body and began dragging it through the shit.

"Hayley is fucking crazy. You have no idea. Everybody in this camp knows. You can't trust her at all. She will do anything to turn people against me at this point."

I closed my eyes and let his filth cover me, bathing in his cruelty while running over the hundreds of times I had let him into my skin.

"You know why I give Hayley no work and I never help her as a songwriter? 'Cause she doesn't fucking focus. She's more concerned with what goes in her mouth than what goes on the fucking microphone."

I reached out and pressed the space bar. I scrolled back and played that part again.

"You know why I give Hayley no work and I never help her as a songwriter? 'Cause she doesn't fucking focus. She's more concerned with what goes in her mouth than what goes on the fucking microphone."

I reached out and pressed the space bar. I scrolled back and played it again.

I took out my phone and recorded a voice note of his words and saved them under "You'll need this."

tal

say i didn't

As I lay on my bed in Silver Lake, my phone lit up. NOPE calling.

I stared at it. Quiet and still, careful not to make any sudden movements like it was a growling lion at the foot of my bed. I shoved my hands under me and pushed myself against my headboard, creating as much space as possible between us.

It rang and rang and rang and stopped.

A few minutes went by, then my phone lit up again. NOPE calling.

The lion grinned at the foot of my bed, licking his paws and rubbing his head against the wall, inviting me to pet him.

A few minutes later, it lit up one more time. NOPE calling. The lion rolled onto his back, legs in the air, weak and hungry, begging me to rub his belly. I pulled my hands out from under me; crawled over; ran my fingers through his soft, thick fur; and picked up the phone.

"Hi, Tal. Welcome back. What's up?" I said.

I was still very much signed to him professionally but was making real efforts to remove myself from any sort of social or personal involvement.

He had this extraordinary ability to make me speechless, hypnotized by his spiralling monologues that guilted and manipulated me into agreeing to see him. I knew it was cultivated over years of making me feel weak and small. I knew it was born in a place where I was new to L.A. and didn't know anybody but him, but it didn't really matter that I could name it at that point. What mattered was that it had the same effect. Just because I understood the addiction, that didn't magically give me the tools to combat it, unfortunately. Just because a person knows they're addicted to crack doesn't miraculously give them the ability to sit in a crack house and feel calm and in control.

He began a long, tangled diatribe, dipping in and out of kindness, then turning in an instant to hurt me, all the while lobbying for me to get in my car and come over. He could talk uninterrupted for literally hours, what must have been millions of words, while I listened and paced and said almost nothing. In these trances, hanging up didn't even cross my mind.

I had just started dating someone new. A sweet southern songwriter new to L.A. named Max. I pictured his sparkly green eyes and huge smile and way-too-long-for-his-body arms and started whispering, "No."

"I'm not coming over, Tal."

"I'm not coming over."

"I'm not coming over."

In the same way he refused to hear my noes, I refused to stop saying it. His anger escalated in swarming insults and bullying rage and professional threats. Then it cut out in the sudden violent silence of being hung up on.

I stood up and looked down at the now chained and frightened lion lying at my feet. I leaned in as close as I could. With the chain holding him against the wall, I screamed in his face, letting all my bottled-up anger cover his shivering, dominated body.

I woke up the next morning to a text from NOPE. *I'm sorry about last night. I shouldn't have tried to pressure you after you told me about Max. Why don't you come by the studio later and play me what you've been working on this last couple of weeks. There's a bunch of producers I wanna introduce you to.*

He had apologized to me on maybe four other occasions over the five years he had been fucking me, so it felt authentic and I believed him.

Molly and her pregnant belly were a month away from making the big move from Canada, so I had been trying to keep my distance in the time leading up to that.

As I was on my way to the studio later that evening, he texted me: *We worked out of the house today so just come here.* I drove up his winding driveway like I had done a hundred times before. The door open, I walked in to hear him yelling from the studio, "Back here." I walked around the corner in my gym shorts and a beaten-up hoodie to find him sitting at the computer, editing vocals on a track.

I sat down on a rolling chair behind him. He swivelled around to look at me, leaned in, and wrapped his hand around my shoe. Laughing uncomfortably, I uncrossed my legs, taking my filthy sneaker out of his hand.

He said, "Have you heard the new one yet? It's insane." He reached to turn it on.

Before it started, I said, "I'm gonna grab some water."

The song began playing as I left the room.

I walked into the kitchen to grab an Evian from his always-stocked fridge. By the time I closed the fridge door, he was standing behind me, his chest pressed against my back. He pushed me against the fridge and began running his hands under my sweater.

I aggressively pulled them out and said, "No. I'm not doing this."

He ran his hand down the back of my shorts and pushed his fingers into me.

Pulling his hand out, I said again, "No. I can't do this. You have to stop."

Growling into my ear like he wasn't at all registering the words coming out of my mouth, he began pulling my shorts down.

I dropped the water bottle, grabbed my waistband with both hands to pull them back up, and said again, "Tal, no."

He said, "Hayley, yes."

He managed to pull my shorts out of my hands and I felt him hard against my skin. I moved quickly out of the way, shifting to the corner where the kitchen counters met. He pulled my shorts back down and leaned me over the counter, slipping his fingers into me again.

I pressed my hands against the counter as he adjusted his body and began pushing himself into me.

"Tal, no."

"Hayley, yes."

"Tal, no."

"Hayley, yes."

Eventually, I just stopped saying no.

He walked me to his bedroom, slipped a condom on, and pulled me on top of him.

A thousand miles away, I felt him throbbing beneath me.

Dizzy and disoriented and disappointed in myself, I came.

He finished, then went into the ensuite bathroom.

Feeling like I was going to throw up, I stood and pulled my shorts on the way you do after a pelvic exam, quickly and sexlessly, not wanting a doctor or the next patient who suspects she has a urinary tract infection to accidently walk in.

He joined me in the kitchen a few minutes later, adjusting his pants and pulling a fresh shirt over his tanned chest. I started getting my stuff together to leave.

"Say I didn't rape you," he said.

I froze, still and outside of myself.

He said again, "I didn't rape you. Say I didn't rape you."

I stayed silent. Hovering over my body, looking down at my tender shape.

"You were saying no, but you were kind of saying yes. In the future, if you really don't want a guy to touch you, just walk out. You're strong — just leave."

I nodded as I picked up my keys from his kitchen counter.

"Let's go for a walk before you go, at least. You don't have to leave right this second."

Obedient and exhausted, I put my things on the table, and we began walking down the street to Yogurtland. We walked along Colfax, the headlights streaking together into bright, endless streams of light.

I picked up an empty cup and stood silently in front of the towering wall of flavours while he babbled about songwriting and filled his cup with mango sorbet. A laughing couple, connected at the pelvis, wiggled past me, taking turns filling their cups with chocolate–peanut butter swirl.

I stepped up to the vanilla lever and pulled it down. Making no effort to circle the cup in order to make a perfect swirl. I walked past the toppings and put my dessert on the scale next to Tal's mango sorbet. The pubescent cashier dropped a pink spoon into mine and a blue spoon into Tal's, then thanked us for choosing Yogurtland.

We walked back through the stainless neighbourhood. Windows lit up, silhouetting happy families having dinner and watching TV. He babbled about how good my new songs were, perhaps trying to balance the scales with flattery and insincere support.

Back at his place, I grabbed my things and threw out my untouched dessert. I got in my car and drove home, thinking, *He didn't rape you. Say he didn't rape you.*

tal

things you do at night

On the nights the cleaning lady wasn't coming by and enough of the regulars were gone, Tal and I would fuck in the vocal booth, my face and chest and arms pushed up against the spongy black soundproofing, or we'd just fold down the couch and turn on a YouTube D'Angelo music video and do it there. The black leather gripped onto our skin as the room filled with moisture. When we were done, he'd toss me the container of baby wipes and I'd clean up the scene, wedging the scented sheets into the black post-coital cracks.

At this point, I was gone. I had killed off any remaining shreds of moral consideration. I had become completely disassociated, looking down from above, shaking my head in disapproval. I felt damaged and helpless, so why not test my threshold? Why not flick a lighter and push the hot metal against the back of my neck? Why not see how long I could let the tiny flame burn before pressing it just under my hairline, singeing a few innocent little blond hairs and leaving a quiet, oval, pink swollen stamp?

On nights the cleaning lady was coming by, we got creative. Molly had just made the move to live full-time in Los Angeles, so we couldn't go to his place anymore, because wife and family. And we couldn't go to mine, because roommates and shame. So we started tracing the soft, subtle, seductive skin of the next incarnation of our affair with a little field trip.

I had been sitting in the common room for most of the day, checking emails, listening to my shitty demos of my shitty songs, and watching *Frasier* with my headphones on. When someone walked by, I would speedily close the Netflix window and open a Word document, wanting people to at least think I was working. Like anyone cared.

Tal came out of his room and, without stopping, walked by the entrance to the lounge, turning his head to say, "Let's go." Obedient, I pushed my things into my bag as quickly as possible, rushing after him in the hopes of catching him in a kind mood.

By the time I got out the front door, he was idling in his Audi, waiting for me to get in. I hopped into the passenger side and waited for him to look up from his phone and acknowledge that another person was in the car. A few minutes later, he turned on whatever song he had been working on all day and started driving while speaking in my general direction.

I had a feeling I knew where we were going when he started driving north on Coldwater Canyon. I knew from the conversations I'd heard in the common room, conversations I'd expressed interest in — in part to be one of the guys and in part out of genuine curiosity.

We pulled into a lot, a small neon sign flickering in the rear-view mirror as we parked. As we walked toward a large bouncer dude, Tal pulled out a wad of cash and motioned over his shoulder at me. The bouncer took the cash from his hand and pushed open a heavy black door, letting us into the dark, nearly empty strip club. A few scattered, still, silhouetted men watched a topless dancer lying on her back, her legs in the air pressed against a thin steel pole, the men's hot breath, flushed cheeks, and steadily tightening pants confirming her night's paycheque.

Tal led me to a table in the middle of the room. Far enough back to keep us from sharing any of the stage light. To keep our faces shadowed and our identities blurred.

He leaned over, pushing his warm lips against my ear, and said, "Do you think she's sexy?"

I turned to look at him, my eyes only a few inches from his, piercing through the beams of light that created pools of cold yellow on the dozen or so tables and carpeted floors. I nodded my head and said, "Yes."

We sat in silence and watched her stretch and bend and reach like a kitten just waking up. The song ended a few minutes later, and she switched back into pedestrian mode, clumsily collecting ones and fives from the front of the stage.

He stood up and, without looking at me, said, "Let's go."

I followed him out of the moist, thick, throbbing club and back into the parking lot.

I stared at myself in the mirror on the passenger side, something I generally tried not to do when I was with him. Split in two, the sane, strong woman inside my head watching the flailing, quiet, desperate woman pressed against the leather, her face lit by flashes of city lights and high beams.

In these moments beside him I was entirely resigned, incapable of seeing my agency in any of it. In these moments, the thought was, *Well, I've already fucked today up. I'll figure out how to get better tomorrow. I'll find a way out tomorrow.* In these moments I was simultaneously terrified at the thought of him dropping me back off at my car, like a punishment, and of spending one more night putting my body in danger under his.

We drove south on Coldwater until we hit Ventura. We turned right, passing gaggles of restaurant patrons parking their cars; bar-goers stumbling out of heavy wooden doors, draped over each other; young couples on first dates; old couples on old dates.

He pulled into a beat-up beige complex. The *L* and *G* and *O* burnt out on the neon sign, causing it to read *Famin Lodge* rather than *Flamingo.* I sat in his idling Audi as he coolly slid out of the driver's seat to work out a room with the receptionist. A three-hundred-year-old woman in a fluorescent-lit, stand-alone front-desk booth in the middle of the parking lot.

I shifted my feet, rearranging his collection of almost-empty water bottles and protein-bar wrappers and cash. I watched them stand in the booth and thought, *These two creatures would never have crossed paths if not for tonight.* Thought, *If this were a painting and it wasn't clear that it was a motel, what theories might a young art student have as to what this salty pair are up to?*

He reached out his hand and took a rectangular white room key from the tentacles of the gatekeeper, then slinked out of the fluorescence and back to the car. He pulled up ten feet or so, having to back in and out a few times to wedge his expensive car in the tiny parking space beside a beat-up maroon Nissan.

I walked behind him toward room 8, compulsively looking over my shoulder in a way he never did. Completely terrified that someone might see me, I turned my face into his sweater as he swiped the key. The tiny green light blinked, gaining us access, and I followed him into the dark, musky little room.

This became a habit for a couple months. His seventy-five bucks buying us seven hours in a room, one or two of which we'd use.

I stayed there one night after he had gone home. I lay on my back, naked in the cum-stained sheets, running through the rest of his night in real time. "He's getting into his car, pulling out of the parking lot. He's turning left up Colfax. Turning right past the canyon. He's pressing the button to open the gate, driving up the winding driveway, and parking behind the white BMW he bought her. He's unlocking the front door. She's tiptoeing out of the bedroom beside theirs, her finger over her lips as if to say, *Shhhh, he just fell asleep.* He's dropping his bag in the living room, brushing his teeth in the hall bathroom, and walking into their bedroom. She's sitting on the right side of the bed, humming into the pastel-green bassinet. She's reaching down to click on the mobile attached to the side of the crib, quietly telling the tiny fabric planets to begin spinning overhead. He's pushing the hair off of her shoulders and kissing the tip of her spine. She's sighing. He's leaning back and plugging in his phone. He'll be sound asleep in three, two, one."

I reached over to grab my phone, knowing there was no one I could call who I wouldn't have to lie to. Instead, I wrapped myself in a towel, flipped my phone on its side, turned on *Friends*, watched eight episodes in a row, passed out for two hours, then drove home before the sun came up.

tal

unfurnished business

"Let's try this room tonight." Tal walked ahead of me, stepping into an empty room in the empty house he'd just bought as a rental property. The room looked out onto a pile of lumber, which would one day become a patio. There was an open can of paint in the corner, and bright-blue tape still lined the creases of the walls and protected the doorknobs from curious, wandering specks of white. Tal reached to open a window so we wouldn't get dizzy from the paint fumes and cleaning supplies.

He pulled his jacket off.

Some family I don't know must live there now. Some kid must be throwing a Frisbee, lodging it in the giant fig tree beside the garage. Some couple must be using that room as a den, or a nursery, maybe. It's a good size for a baby's room and just across the hall from the master bedroom, making it easy for the parents to slip exhaustedly out of bed and comfort their sobbing infant.

Tal did this thing where he would sort of hum against my ear, then jokingly make out with me for a second before really turning it on. He kind of growled into my neck, then motioned for me to lie on the ground. He took his shirt off and glanced at his own reflection in the window.

Nobody knew where I was. Nobody in the entire world knew I was there, on that floor, on that Wednesday night.

I looked up at the ceiling as he disappeared between my legs and I hated myself. I particularly hated myself on nights like this one, when I drove myself there. Nights like this one when a plan needed to be agreed on, times needed to be set, addresses and alarm codes and teamwork. All of that self-hatred made my need for my orgasm even stronger. It was the only way out for the night, even if just for a minute.

I leaned into how much my back hurt as my spine dug into the hardwood floor, and I looked around the room as he pressed his body up against mine. I left my eyes open intentionally, like the disgusting nature of this scene was sort of the point at this stage in our affair. The paint chips that stuck to my bare ass and the dangling, unfinished light fixture are what kept me there. It had to be bad in order to survive it. The dingier it was, the better — the more I could lodge it into a quiet, private part of my brain, where it could cuddle with all my other weird impulses. It could snuggle up against that wiggly feeling I get in my knees standing on a thirtieth-floor balcony. It could open its disgusting arms and embrace the little voice that tells those wiggly knees how easy it would be to jump. It could keep all my existing shame company, and nobody in there would judge it. It could chill on a chair next to that time I tried to fuck myself with an electric toothbrush, or when I broke into Cye's house when we were no longer together, or when I told my best friend she only got the part in the high-school musical because they couldn't give me the lead six years in a row. It could relax freely with all my other unkind moments and flawed decisions and the bits of my personality I am afraid of. Because if I started seeing this as good, then it would slip into the part of my brain where love lives. Then that would become love. That would become what I wanted and what I would inevitably look for in someone else when Tal and I were finally done on some perfect day somewhere in the future.

He finished and pecked my cheek, then walked out of the room to run a shower.

I stayed on the ground with my pants off for a few minutes longer than I needed to. I floated up above my body to clock this, hoping I could capture enough of this shame in one snapshot to call this the final addition to a folder I'd been building in my head, titled "Enough, Hayley."

I pulled my pants on and joined him in the bathroom. I washed my hands, then brushed my teeth with my finger, not because I wanted to particularly, but because otherwise, why was I in the bathroom? This was not a sweet, intimate, loving, giggle-at-each-other's-reflections-in-the-mirror type of moment.

He was only showering because he would be in bed with Molly an hour later.

And I would be home, thinking about how I shouldn't have broken up with Max and lied to my roommate, telling him things went late at the studio.

Tal's tenants were moving in a few days later, so we would have to find somewhere else to go. Or maybe this really was the last time — a thought that was both exhilarating and terrifying.

me

marbles

I have a major issue with marbles. I can't have them around me. I didn't always feel this way. Growing up, my good friend Anna had a marble run and we would spend hours perching the tiny, opaque glass eyes at the top of the run, then watching them expertly fall through the coloured tubes. The marble was a versatile toy. It came in a number of sizes and colours. Black or white or rainbow or almost as if it had cataracts or a lightning bolt had struck right through it. It could be rolled down a set of stairs or slingshot at the neighbour you had a crush on or used to line the floor under the welcome mat at your house, ensuring your brother and his friends would wipe out.

I was nine; my sister Danica was six. We were playing in my bedroom — my bedroom with the giant mural of a tiger's face on the wall — next to the bathroom. Our babysitter's muted voice drifted across the hall as she rocked our youngest sister, Kendra, to sleep. Danica and I kept our voices down, afraid to disturb the nap ritual. We sat against the wall, fishing loose marbles out of a pencil case filled with coloured markers.

I want to say I was wearing a long-sleeved white shirt with a number of vibrant dinosaur patches sewn onto it. I want to say Danica was in a navy-blue jumpsuit. I also want to place us in front of Grandma's closet, though I know this memory did not take place in that room. The clips of home videos we do have tend to overlay the memories that we have no video footage for. My photographed outfits drape over the faceless memories and help piece together a visual of my life.

I found a giant transparent marble hiding under a fat yellow highlighter. I fished it out and followed the same instinct I'd had when Kendra was born, when I put her tiny hand in my mouth, buffered my teeth with my lips, and softly gnawed her palm. I pulled the endlessly smooth marble out of the plastic case and placed it against my tongue, just for a second, looking at Danica with a glisten of *I know this isn't a good idea* in my eyes.

She said, "Spit it out. You're gonna choke." I egged on her fear by bringing the marble back up to my mouth, running it along my lips, teasing her. I placed it on my tongue again as she begged, "Take it out of your mouth. You're gonna choke!"

I smiled playfully at Danica. Then the marble did what marbles do best: it slid perfectly along my tongue, effortlessly corking my throat in one heavy plop.

I wrapped my hands around my neck and tried to scream, tried to scream like trying to run away from someone in a nightmare. Tried and failed. Danica started yelling as I got up and ran across the hall into my parents' room, where Christine was putting Kendra to sleep. I pointed to my throat and pounded on my chest as the light in the room faded as if on a dimmer. I felt myself getting light-headed. Without hesitating, Christine wound up and hit me as hard as she could in the centre of my back (a lesser-used alternative to the Heimlich manoeuvre). The marble shot out of my mouth, bounced off my parents' dresser, and landed perfectly between Danica and me on the beige carpet.

A small wooden bowl sits on my bedside table, one of the many gifts from Daniel's thanks-for-the-fuck Emmy gift bag. It's filled with a variety of stones, each claiming to assist in something from love to sex to psychic powers. I didn't buy any of these stones. I sort of accumulated them over the years, like 100 percent of women in L.A. do.

Sometimes this wave of temptation pours over me. I'll be lying in bed, running an orb of quartz over my eyes, praying for some dude to love me again. Then I'll realize how close my eyes are to my mouth, how easy it would be to part my lips and place the stone against my tongue. Like, maybe this time it won't slip. Maybe this time I can tempt fate for a second longer. Some nights, I look around the room, though I am well aware nobody can see me in my small bachelor apartment, then open my mouth and start by licking it. Just quickly. Like, "Look, you don't control me." Then I tip my head forward so gravity can't drop the stone down my throat, and I push the whole thing into my mouth. The second my lips close around it, I spit it back out.

So this is why I shouldn't have marbles around.

Unfortunately, I have kept men like this, like marbles. Men I know will hurt me. Men I can just casually slip onto my tongue, then spit out when they've shown me I'm alive by reminding me how close I am to death.

duckie

unrequited-ish

Unrequited love sucks. Its sucking, however, has yet to deter me from jumping in wholeheartedly when I sense the slightest hint of disinterest.

We all have long games. The people you tuck into the corner of your heart and head, the relationships that haven't fully metastasized yet — and may never.

I carried Duckie like that. Like a small concerning lump tucked beside my left breast. I ran my fingers over it, comforted by the absolute assurance that at some point it would require my full attention.

I had been under Tal's spell for basically as long as I had known Duckie. Duckie was under a similar spell, which allowed me to feel grounded, almost safe. Like I had someone in the cell with me. Five full years of conversations surrounded the subject, years of "I don't feel the same way," years of "This is never gonna happen," years of "It's just too complicated." Years that only just recently got me to a place where I was ready to make peace with it. To ask the surgeon to remove the cyst, to stare at it in a metal bowl on a hospital counter, all bloody and calcified. To thank it for encouraging me to live my life with urgency, and then to tip it into the trash with the rest of the heartbreaks and other love-related illnesses.

We started that day at the coffee shop down the street from Duckie's house studio. Duckie bought me my soy chai and his usual, a luxurious iced caramel latte, the silky whole milk tenderly contributing to his perfect little belly.

I slipped a skinny red straw into his drink, a weekly ritual that somehow felt intimate, touching the tip of his straw moments before it touched his lips. I watched his mouth purse, feeling ever so slightly responsible for the look of satisfaction on his face as the drink moved down his throat.

We spent the afternoon in Duckie's studio, writing a pop song for an artist, a quick, easy session I don't need to spend time going over here. All you really need to know is that when Duckie and I are together, we laugh. We laugh a lot. We bring out the best in each other, the parts that are playful and understanding and supportive. We know when the other is losing interest or hungry or tired. We know when the other has given up on the song or is just suggesting lyrics to get out of the room. I know him.

We finished the session and ate a quick dinner accompanied by a few mezcal mules in a few chilled copper mugs. I had been texting with an ex throughout the evening and was planning a late-night booty call, so I attempted to say good night.

"No, stay. Let's smoke a joint and watch something."

The combination of weed, a movie, and Duckie was almost impossible for me to say no to, so I stayed. I sat on the couch the way I always did, the corner spot almost perfectly the shape of my ass at that point. I curled up, preparing for our usual routine: a movie, a joint, a snack, me safely on one couch and him on the other, creating enough space to absolutely ensure that nothing unsavoury could happen.

I sat there for a moment before he asked me to go listen to something he had been working on in the studio. He had been in Tal's band of individually brilliant musicians as long as I'd known him and had just started quietly working on his own project, a project he was terrified to share with anyone but me.

I sat beside him, in a rolling chair with a me-shaped ass print similar to the one on the couch, and listened to him pour his heart out in song form. This cinematic eruption, like Thom fucked Trent while Björk watched.

He pulled out a guitar and started playing me a new progression he had been working on. This beautiful plucking melody he didn't know what to do with. I heard where it needed to go and started playing the rest of it as if it were already written.

I tracked the guitar part, then we rolled our rolly chairs toward the microphone and started singing together, something we always struggled to do without laughing hysterically. I was usually laughing because I was hyperaware of the distance between our lips, our fingers, our eyes. I imagine he was laughing because funny noises are funny.

After a stupid number of takes, we decided to call it quits. For some reason I brought up a recent video I had taken of him, a video where he looked exactly like his father.

He got quiet, looked at me, and said, "I wanna kiss you."

In a genuine moment of pure surprise, my mouth moved without me, totally separate from my body, how dirty my hair was, how stupid my outfit. It said, "What?"

He rolled his chair over to me and leaned in. A lean I had been dreaming about, measuring, quietly manifesting for five full years. We kissed, his tongue dipping between my lips. I reached up and put my hand on his cheek, feeling his jaw open and shut around me. Pulling back for a moment, he looked at me like a terrified child, then fell into my arms, holding me so tight.

He kissed my neck. I pressed my hand against the back of his head as I ran my wet lips along his ear, his shoulder, his chin, kissing him in the way I'd wanted to for so long. And I could feel his heart beating in his throat against my fingertips and I could smell the subtle corner of whisky on his breath and trace the clean red sunburn line on his shoulder with my pinky.

And I reached down to feel him hard against my palm, just on the other side of the thinnest layer of fabric. He ran his huge, gorgeous hands up my legs, squeezing my calves and tensing around my upper thighs. Then he stopped and said, "Let's not have sex tonight. I just … this is … I can't. It's too much."

With the space usually occupied by the elephant in the room now occupied by touch, we sat, tangled in each other, and talked. We talked about how long it had taken us to get there. Talked about how much we'd both thought about it. How crazy it was that it hadn't happened already. How maybe we should just start a family.

I held his hands, realizing I had been inches away from those hands for years and had never touched them. I massaged his feet, quietly worshipping his body, now hyperaware of how overwhelmed he was, so used to not connecting with someone who really knows him, someone who really sees him, someone he can't hide from.

We started watching videos of old songs on YouTube: James Taylor, Neil Young, Joni Mitchell. Laughing at our shared theory that Joni sounds like a didgeridoo when she climaxes.

The issue with connecting with someone you know really well is that there is no hiding. There was nothing he could do to fool me. I saw him clearly. I felt him clearly. So, as 2:00 a.m. approached, as I was running my fingers over his back, I felt his temperature change. It was so subtle, I wondered if he even recognized it, the tiniest adjustments in his movements that screamed, *I'm terrified*.

"Listen, let's go lie in your bed for ten minutes, then I'll sleep on the couch 'cause you're gonna have a full-blown panic attack if you wake up next to me in the morning," I said.

He nodded like a child. He nodded like I had just opened the closet in his bedroom and said, "See, there are no monsters in here."

We walked to his room and quickly took turns brushing our teeth in the bathroom. We lay in his bed, my head on his chest, feeling his heart start to burrow away from the surface. Feeling it quietly try to find somewhere to hide, somewhere I wouldn't think to look.

I sat up, leaned over him, and kissed him four times, his tongue pulling farther away from my mouth on each pulse.

I got up and walked out.

I think he said good night. Good night like goodbye.

Around 7:00 a.m. he emerged from his cave to get something out of the fridge. I lifted my hand in the air and reached for him. I reached for him to touch me. I reached for him to give me a single moment of contact before going back into his room, to tell me with a single action that we were okay.

He walked past my arm.

And, lying on the couch, I heard his door shut.

Trying hard to push the reality of his morning regret into my peripherals, I left his house, wanting to be gone by the time he got up. I was so concerned with how he was handling the morning, I wasn't even glancing at my own relationship to the magnitude of the night.

I got a series of texts shortly after, texts attempting to convince me that he felt nothing, that this wasn't right for him, and that the massive panic attack he'd had that morning was somehow a reflection of me. That if it were right, he would have felt something else, something different.

My heart caved in the way it always does with heartbreak, but this time was different. This time it wasn't rejection that hurt me. I hadn't asked him for anything. I had given him no question to say no to.

In a single stroke, he repainted the entire night. He reshaped it in the image of his fear. He jumped back in time and redirected the entire scene. He created space where there was none; he added uncomfortable side glances, pursed lips, closed bodies.

He stole the night from me. He ripped this fresh, soft, beautiful memory from my hands, like a baby from a mother's arms. This night we had been marching toward for five full years.

The issue with connecting with someone you know really well is that there is no hiding. There was nothing he could do to fool me. I saw him clearly. I felt him clearly.

At least I thought I did.

I'd been through enough shitty nights with shitty men not kissing me back and enough incredible nights with incredible men pulling me close that I knew the difference.

Or at least I thought I did.

So, I had a choice to make.

I could choose to believe him, or I could reject my cognitive dissonance and double down, continuing with my stubborn belief that he must love me, regardless of the damning evidence otherwise.

Like, how could my body be that wrong? How could my gut be that off?

duckie

olive juice

There's a long waterway that flows through the valley, through North Hollywood to Glendale, where it takes a hard-right turn through downtown to eventually meet up with Long Beach. I know very little about it. Only that it's sometimes full and sometimes empty and sometimes somewhere in between. Only that it would be very easy to climb down into and very hard to climb up out of.

I walk along it like I did the canals in London. I stop to look at birds or pick up shiny trash or whisper "It won't last" to couples in love passing by. In my experience, it is best to be close to water when having any kind of difficult conversation. It's best to sit beside something that is constantly changing, something that, the next time you visit it, will be different, perhaps ensuring you can never revisit the scene of the crime, not exactly. Perhaps reminding you of the constantly morphing nature of things.

I messaged Duckie the evening of August 28, after watching his charged silhouette walk out of my show in the middle of a new song I had written about him. A loving farewell of a song called "Olive Juice," which was birthed out of the piece we started together that night at his place. I had watched him reach for the exit like a life raft, gasping for air, half-lit by the bar. I had watched the door close slowly behind him at the back of the packed room, as the audience erupted in applause. His body disappeared behind the glass in the background while I stared into the blinding stage lights and began introducing the next song.

It had been exactly one month since our night together.

I messaged him after the show and suggested we talk on the phone at eleven the following morning. Now, after twenty minutes of walking along the waterway, rehearsing the points I wanted to hit, practising key phrases I thought were particularly poignant, referencing past conversations, and creating a bullet-proof case against him and his behaviour — not only the night of my show but the morning after our night together — I began looking for an unoccupied bench to nest on.

I passed many that were unoccupied, but they weren't quite right. The sort of conversation I was about to have deserved the perfect bench. A bench appealing enough that I'd want to hover there for what could be up to an hour, but not so nice that I'd want to revisit it anytime soon. A bench where I could watch the lazy water sluggishly flow by in the half-full waterway, where I could be shaded and still feel the broken-up light streaming between families of leaves. A bench that was private but close enough to Ventura that I could hear the cars humming by, reminding me that I was not alone.

I sat down on what I deemed to be the perfect bench, shifting onto my right hip, ignoring the pain in my back from some herniated disks. Pain that, in my usual way, I'd been pretending wasn't there for almost a year. I looked down at my phone: 10:47.

In thirteen minutes, I would call him, or he'd call me.

In thirteen minutes, we would talk for the last time.

Looking at my phone every minute or so, I slipped into my memories of Duckie. I ran backward and met him again for the first time, in his dad's basement, five years before. I closed my eyes, feeling the broken-up light turn my face into a weepy mosaic, and disappeared into the first moment I saw him.

I reached out my hand and knocked on his dad's door in Toronto. This was the morning I met him, in a blind producer-writer date, a couple months before we both moved to L.A. I knocked and looked down at my phone. Hearing the door open, I looked up and came face to face with his father, a taller, heavier, warm-once-you-get-to-know-him kind of guy. My favourite kind of guy. The kind whose affection is earned.

He yelled, "Hayley's here."

"Be right up," Duckie shouted from the basement. The sound of his voice washing over me like an old friend, already familiar and familial.

"You want something to drink?" his father asked.

We walked toward the kitchen, past the soft, clean, adulty, personality-less living room and all its photos of his modern family. He poured me a glass of water while we waited for his son to emerge.

Leaning against the doorway at the top of the stairs, I heard Duckie run up behind me. Skipping two stairs at a time, then doing the last three in one long leap.

"Hi, Hayley. How are you? Nice to meet you."

I loved him right away. His low, heavy voice, like running a warm bath; his broad shoulders and huge, thick hands; his wide nose and sleepy blue eyes. His imperfect skin, a few subtle indentations, scars from high-school acne, quietly showing me that at some point he did not find himself desirable. A trait that made me like him even more. A trait that made me want to hug him right away. That made me want to cry with him right away. That made me want to hold his face in my hands and tell him how beautiful he was right away.

His dad passed me a tall, cool glass of water and left us to it.

I walked down the stairs behind Duckie. Stepping on the three he had skipped, causing a loud creak. I then realized he had skipped over those steps intentionally, exposing how well his body knew this staircase, how many hundreds of times he had run up and down them, always avoiding those three creaking steps. I smiled secretly behind him, already comforted by recognizing something so ingrained. Already feeling like I had been let in on an intimate habit. Perhaps something even his family didn't realize he did.

Ten fifty-two. In eight minutes I'd call him, or he'd call me. In eight minutes, we'd talk for the last time.

I closed my eyes again and met him on our secret beach. The one near Malibu. The one we had to climb over a cliff to get to. The one hidden just on the other side of the rocks. Past the playing families and tanning couple who thought they'd found the best spot.

I zoomed in on us lying side by side in the sand on the beach blanket I left in my trunk year-round. The blanket I'd bought at a garage sale with him. I zoomed in on his face next to mine. On my bathing suit zipped open to my belly button, dangerously open.

I zoomed in on us belting "You're Still the One" by Shania Twain into the crisp blue sky. On his fat bottom lip shaping the words, his hand reaching above us to conduct the lengthy chorus harmony like he always did.

I zoomed in on him laughing, rolling his head over to look at me, his blond hair speckled with sparkling sand, and his sleepy blue eyes squinting shut.

Ten fifty-eight. In two minutes, I'd call him. Or he'd call me. Either way, in two minutes we would talk for the last time.

I closed my eyes again and fell into that moment at the studio, cozied tightly a couple years into my Tal captivity. The moment I came around the corner with Tal and Duckie looked at me from the back of a busy room and shook his head in disappointment. Disappointment in my not knowing how to escape yet. Disappointment to see me, really. To see me still in so much pain. To see me still so trapped.

I saw him shaking his head, giving up on me.

I shook my own head aggressively to change the memory. *No, not that one. Give me another one, please.*

I flipped back through time again and found us in a beat-up car I had borrowed from a friend. I flipped further back to find us driving to Anaheim to see John Mayer.

The memories started flooding from there.

Playing Heads Up! for hours in Boulder in our pyjamas.

The flight when he gave up his business-class ticket to sit with me in coach.

Playing Frisbee in that park by his house.

Walking to get our hundredth coffee at the café around the corner.

The way he called my sister Kendro.

Climbing endless golden sand dunes in Joshua Tree.

That New Year's Eve I was pissed at him.

That New Year's Eve I wasn't.

How he called me that time he couldn't find his new puppy. How he panicked and thought of me. How I reached my bare fingers behind his toilet, risking the claws and teeth of a frightened animal for him.

How, for a minute there, I was his emergency contact. Of the dozen or so we each have in our life, I was one of his, regardless of what insignificance he wants to assign that.

Holding his hand as we walked out of his eye surgery. His clutching my arm, trusting me to not walk him into traffic.

I looked down and saw the tiny scar on my right big toe and remembered how I accidentally kicked his metal patio set that time we were smoking weed with his roommate in the backyard. How they stood over me, eating ice cream out of a cardboard carton as I bled and laughed on his bathroom floor.

And finally. Back to that night, exactly a month earlier. The night he had looked up at me and said, "I wanna kiss you."

Eleven o'clock.

My phone rang.

"Hi," I said.

"Hey," he said.

We launched into it pretty quickly, too deep in the shit to pretend we weren't. Maybe I thought this conversation would make things better. Maybe I thought it would fix things in some way, or maybe I just needed to express my disappointment. Shake my head at him from the back of a room at his unwillingness to escape.

Or maybe I just needed to say goodbye.

He said two things I don't know how to forgive him for.

He told me the mood had been so right that night that I could have been anyone. That he would have felt something for anyone. That my me-ness was the least influential variable of the night. That perhaps the mezcal mules were to blame.

And he said, "Hayley, I just don't understand why you stuck around me for so long, when you knew I never felt the way you do. Like, you knew this was going to happen if you stayed around long enough. And you could have said no to me."

I clutched the side of the bench, crying and laughing and nauseated. All of a sudden, he and Tal bled together. Their words joining in perfect unison, their bodies intertwined.

By being in this room, you get what you get.

And suddenly I flew back into Tal's kitchen and heard him say, "If you really don't want a guy to touch you, just walk out. You're strong — just leave."

My heart cracked cleanly down the middle, like a coconut, in a way that didn't even hurt. In a way that was so deep and so reshaping that I watched it with shock rather than sadness.

In that moment I closed my eyes and watched this tiny blue core memory plop into existence. I watched it roll up into my mind's headquarters, into the bulletproof-glass trophy case, and take its place next to the collection of other impenetrable defining words and events.

"Well, that's probably good for me then. I'm gonna hang up now," I said.

"Just know, like, I'll always wish good things for you," he said.

"Yeah. Okay." I hung up.

I put my phone back into my pocket. Noticing the waterway had filled up during our call. Noticing the world already looked different.

tal ᵕᐧᵕ arthur

let's all pretend together

I asked Tal's production partner, Arthur, to meet me at this hole-in-the-wall coffee shop in Van Nuys. I sat down at the only patio table, its cheap, flimsy body teetering a couple feet from the busy, speeding traffic on Burbank. Though, I would have picked that table even if there were other seating options. It would only take one of those speeding drivers making a single wrong move to slip and wipe out the table entirely, and that's how L.A. life always felt — one casual slip away from the end.

I asked Arthur to meet me because I was exhausted. I needed to tell him I was way past feeling safe with Tal. I needed to tell him I was tired of Tal casually slipping his hand down the front of my pants as he walked by. That I was tired of having to physically remove Tal's hands from my body when my noes didn't work.

I needed to tell him I was tired of Tal's luring me into a studio under false pretenses, then pushing his fingers into me while I tried to pull them out. I needed to tell him that I was tired of Tal walking into my solo sessions to sit on a chair a foot away and pull out his dick, displaying his erection against his jeans, like a dare.

Arthur appeared on the corner as I dove headfirst into a wave of nervousness. I realized I was nervous about being honest with someone who knew already. Someone that none of this would come as a real surprise to. Someone whose survival must, on some level, depend on his ability to look the other way.

I ran my fingers up the sides of my this-will-end-up-in-a-whale's-stomach plastic to-go cup. Quietly hoping my environmental disregard would suggest to Arthur that I had no plans of staying in his nearness for any longer than I had to.

"Let me go grab a coffee quickly," he said.

I sat and played with my phone, reviewing my notes. Arthur walked out moments later and sat across from me.

"You gotta come by and see the new studio. It's great," he said.

I launched right into it. "Listen, I asked you to come here because I don't want to be signed to you guys anymore. I don't feel safe with Tal. I am grateful for what you guys have done for me. You started my whole career in this country, and I wouldn't take that back. But I feel like this has gone as far as it can. I can't come to the new studio. I can't be there. And I don't think it's reasonable to expect me to stay signed to someone I now feel physically unsafe around."

He immediately looked different. He looked like an animal who realized he had to protect himself. A bit harder, a bit bigger, a bit sharper.

"I mean, we all know that Tal is a big energy, and I try to stay out of his personal business," he said. "But to say you don't feel safe is very serious."

I could feel my skin go from its normal pink to an undeniable cinnamon-heart red — and not because the sun was blazing down on us, not because I was wearing a black hoodie even though it's most always fry-an-egg-on-the-pavement weather in Van Nuys. I started crying, instinctively, like a dog wagging its tail, without the permission of my brain.

I took a deep breath and quieted my body and wished I could tough this out and show him the last text conversation I'd had with Tal. The conversation that read like this:

> Tal: *We go to the beach tomorrow?*
> Me: *I can't.*
> Tal: *Ok. Hey, wanna do a session tomorrow with Justin Bieber?*
> Me: *Thanks for asking but that's okay. You guys have your chemistry.*
> Tal: *Doesn't exist. Just seeing if you're avoiding me.*

I wanted to explain to him what would have happened if I'd said yes. I wanted him to understand that I would have shown up at Tal's Bieber-free home studio. That he would have cornered me in the living room, across from his son's artwork perched on top of the piano. That I would have said no eight times, then nothing once. That he would have inched me back into his bedroom, laying me down beside his son's crib. That I would have attempted to switch positions, at which point he would have held my arms down and whispered, "You don't get to decide."

I wanted to tell him, in detail, the shit I had been handling for five years, but I didn't. I just cried. Though it did something, I guess. He didn't know how to handle my tears, so he softened. He stopped picking at his croissant, perhaps remembering for a moment that he's a father and a brother and a son. Maybe he surprised himself with a moment of honesty. Knowing deep down inside how true and real all this was.

He said he'd talk to Tal the following day and that they'd discuss letting me out of my contract with them.

A week later. I was staying in a friend's place. A temporary post–Silver Lake stomping ground while I tried to figure out what the fuck to do with my life next. I was in the process of finding somewhere more solid to live because this place was down the street from Tal. I had to look both ways before I left the house in the mornings, then stand on the corner and squint my eyes, trying to make out the identities of the blurry-faced men and women and children in the distance.

Sometimes I'd realize I was looking for him rather than making sure he wasn't there. Sometimes seeing him felt better. Because then I knew where he was, and I knew for sure where he wasn't. I could continue my hike thinking he must be just passing the Yogurtland, that he was probably going to Trader Joe's to get plantain chips or CVS for sinus strips. I could put a confident red pin on his whereabouts, and that made me feel safe.

I lay on my bed, watching *Girls* on the TV that had been in my room when I moved in. My phone starting buzzing on the tacky light-blue fleur-de-lis-patterned comforter that came with the room. Tal texting.

He was offering up his assistance in little grey bubbles. He said he'd talked to Arthur and that this stuff was tricky and would take a long time, but they were willing to let me out of their side of my deal. And he suggested he be the one to help me do it. I thanked him, knowing this was not generosity. This was not a gift.

My phone started ringing. The lion at the foot of my bed subtly tilting his head, begging me to pet him.

I opened my laptop on the stupid blue comforter. I was way past trusting him, so as I reached to answer the phone, I opened a track in GarageBand and pressed record, then put my phone on speaker.

He started in a professional manner. He always did. Because that was his in. Because that's how he burrowed. He would make me feel for a moment like he gave a fuck, and I would eat it up. I would dive in like a kid who'd been waiting for her neglectful father to pick her up on the stoop of her mother's house every Sunday for ten years. He would pull up and offer to buy me an ice cream cone and take me for a spin in his truck and I would be grateful and excited and certain I had my father back.

The first half of his monologue was about how hurt he was that I went to Arthur and not to him. He was hurt that I was making him out to be something he felt he was not.

He seamlessly sprinkled this argument with slippery invitations to come over and fuck him after a hike or after we went to see the label or after breakfast or whenever. Like, "Yes, Hayley, we are happy to help you get out of this deal. Pick your favourite songs, then come over and suck my dick and we'll work on a list of some artists you wanna write for." His suggestions flew by like a speeding train. Like you're standing by the tracks and an open boxcar flashes by and you see a blur of black and white and go, "Was that a train full of cows?" It isn't until you look back and slow down the memory that you can see the giant pile of decomposing cow corpses in perfect detail.

He asked me if I wanted him. Over and over. Each time, I sat silently, then pushed out a "No, Tal." He couldn't hear my noes. He listened and received them for only a fraction of a second before diving right back down into why I was wrong. Why I should be fucking him. Why it wasn't his fault that he was still trying to fuck me at all. Why it was because of some sexual sonar I was sending out that he was merely responding to.

I knew this conversation would be our last. I'd told too many people; I couldn't go back to him now. I'd exposed too much of the truth to make giving in a possibility, and that made this speech sound different. That made this monologue seem sad and unthreatening, like a kid having a temper tantrum.

And I saw my strength, I felt my power.

And it was like I'd been an elephant all along, but I hadn't realized I was an elephant. And I'd been tethered to a wall with a thin fraying rope, but I didn't know it was a rope. It was only in that moment that I realized all I had to do was take one small step away and the rope would snap.

I didn't have to wait for things to get worse.

All I had to do was open my phone and block him.

I opened my phone and blocked him.

ben

closure

"What did your life look like seven years ago, when I lived in Toronto? Before I moved to L.A.?" I asked. We were standing on a street in Toronto's Kensington Market, surrounded by crowded vintage stores and cheap glasses and roti vendors.

Zane and I hadn't known each other back then. He had only just become a casual friend, and I wondered whether there might have been some life overlap before this point. He launched into "I was working there, dating her, watching that. How about you?"

Holding a vegan ice cream cone in my hand, I began telling him about Ben. About how in love I had been. About how,
with some breakups, you see it coming. You watch it walking
steadily in your direction. Tiny at first, in the distance at first,
lit by the setting sun, then nearly at your doorstep by morning.
How for weeks you watch it. But with some breakups, you wake
up, make cinnamon buns, and say, "I don't know if I want coffee
this morning," and he says, "I don't know if I love you anymore."

I was just telling him about Ben's flopsy brown hair and his
permanent morning face, plump and pink and warm, when there
he was, walking steadily in our direction. Ben.

I looked over at Zane and said, "Oh fuck. It's Ben. Oh my
god, please don't see me. Please don't see me."

He walked right up to us and stopped directly in front of me,
the sun behind him, causing beams of light to shoot out around
his permanent morning face and through his flopsy brown hair
as if he had a halo.

"Hi, Ben," I said, getting up to give him a hug. It's impossible
to give Ben a bad hug. He won't allow it. He pulled me in and
held me there like he had nowhere else to be. The sun temporarily blinded me as I rested my chin on his shoulder.

I sat back down and began nervously blabbing. "This is crazy.
I was just talking about you. I asked Zane here — oh yeah, Ben,
Zane, Zane, Ben — I asked him what he was doing seven years
ago. And he was like, 'Yeah, I was working there, dating her. What
about you?' And I was like, 'I was doing' … I mean … you know
what I was doing."

We laughed uncomfortably as I tried desperately to still my
vibrating body.

We small-talked for a few minutes. Work, family. I congratulated
him on his upcoming nuptials, to the first girl he dated after me.
I eventually managed to casually end the conversation by talking
about it like it was already in the past: "It was really good to see you."

I turned back to Zane and attempted to muddle together a sentence while my head spun around the serendipity: Ben and I on the same tiny street in the same tiny market at the exact same moment, when he lives in Nashville and I live in L.A.

Zane had to head to work, so I walked him to his bike. Then I began walking back into the market. I popped into a little vintage shop, casually running my fingers over the rows of jeans as I thought about the chances that Ben and I would be in that same spot at that same time. Given how big the world is and the unfathomable number of events that had to line up just perfectly to make that happen. I took out my phone and started typing his name.

Coffee now? I texted.

He immediately responded. *Fika, on Kensington, I'll be there in five.* I left the store like I was fleeing the scene of a crime, dropping whatever was in my hand and lunging for the door. I began racing back through the market, barely registering the hundreds of people and the jutting-out storefronts and the nuts and the yogurt-covered things.

I came around the corner to find him leaning against the fence in front of the coffee shop. His eyes on his phone, his dark denim jeans thinly covering his perfect cock. I walked slowly toward him. I floated up and off the pavement, suspended midair on the fact that Ben was waiting for me. An event that an hour before would have been unimaginable was suddenly a foot away from me, leaning against a fence in Kensington Market.

I walked up to him and said, "Fuck it, let's do this."

We walked into the cheery Swedish-inspired café. White walls and striped tables and cushions and mugs in various shades of blue. He attempted to get a conversation started as I ordered our drinks. "Ben, I can't half focus on you. Let's just get our drinks, then go sit down."

We took our drinks from the counter and walked through to the back. Quiet panic leaked into my body as I scanned for available seating. I noticed only a couch at first, meaning I would have to sit next to him, pressed against that body I'd collapsed onto hundreds of times, close enough to smell him, to count the subtle effects of aging, the delicate lines around his mouth, the speckled grey in his flopsy brown hair, the sweet fatigue in the purple bags under his eyes. I was about to say, "No fucking way am I sitting next to you on a two-person couch," when a couple stood up, abandoning a picnic table in the corner of the outdoor patio.

We placed our beverages on the table and sat down across from each other like civilized exes. We moved through the easy stuff, work, professional developments, family — the conversations you can have with anybody, the developed monologues you practise over and over again when telling people the story of your life.

Then, with almost no warning, he looked at me like he was about to cry. "I know I have no right to ask you for anything," he said. "But I want you to know, I think about you and it's hard for me to not have you in my life. You're doing so great and I just want to celebrate with you and I can't ... and I know I can't and that's okay."

He anxiously bounced his knee under the table, causing our little world to subtly quake beneath us. He went on, "But it kills me to think that you don't believe I loved you. I did. I still do in a way. We had just stopped growing together. You weren't doing music at all, and I was stuck and didn't know a way out. And again, I know I have no right to ask you for any amount of friendship, but I guess I just want to know that maybe you can envision a future where there could be a bridge built to that place, to that place of being in each other's lives. 'Cause I miss you and I want you in my life and you deserve everything. You deserve to be so loved and it kills me that you haven't been."

Totally overwhelmed, I watched him lay his vulnerability on the picnic table with our empty mugs and mangled napkins, trying very hard not to blink, to keep my welled-up eyes welled up rather than emptied onto my rosy speckled cheeks.

It suddenly occurred to me that I had just received the gift of closure.

I suddenly understood that, at the end of the day, 100 percent of relationships end. Maybe you lose a partner at ninety or get a divorce after thirty years like my parents, or maybe it's just a couple of significant years that feel impossible to get over. But, no matter what, it ends. What matters is feeling significant to each other, being able to move on while simultaneously honouring the time you spent in such precious proximity. The time spent swapping fluids and sharing holidays and bladder infections.

It was nearly impossible to shift back into successful small talk after that. If you had asked me an hour earlier, I would have told you that Ben never thought about me, that he never loved me, and that losing me was in no way a loss. In a single conversation, he challenged everything I thought was true about our entire relationship, almost comically exposing just how much I had made up in the seven years since I broke up with him and the six years since he broke up with me. Exposing just how many decisions I had made based on the false belief that he had never loved me, that I am fundamentally unlovable when I am fully myself.

We picked up our empty mugs and mangled napkins and brought them inside like the polite Canadian patrons we are, dropping them at the counter and thanking the barista with our splotchy red faces.

Face to face, back on Kensington Avenue, the sun now setting around his waist, causing beams of light to shoot out around his brown leather belt, we said goodbye for the last time. And, in a way, said hello for the first time.

enzo

killing my heroes

I woke up to find a long, taut white string tied to the foot of my bed. I followed it up to see a bright-red balloon staring down at me like an ominous hurricane cloud.

Halifax was cold and I was six years old. My uncle Enzo came into my room, lifted one side of my mattress, and shook me onto the hardwood floor of my bedroom in the house on his sprawling oceanside property.

"Follow the string," he said.

I collected myself from the ground, adjusted my pioneer-style nightie, missing only the bonnet, and followed the balloon string to its end, where another, longer string was knotted to it. Looking at Enzo over my shoulder, I tentatively began tiptoeing down the hallway.

The string ran between my fingers as I let it guide me around the house. It dipped me into the kitchen. It slipped in and out of cupboards, through the TV room, into the bathroom, and in and out of the toilet. It ran up the walls and did loops around potted plants in the living room. When it reached the back door, Enzo said, "You're gonna need your boots now."

I pushed my excited bare feet into my garden boots as fast as I could and followed the string down the hill toward the ocean. Halfway to the water, the string led me to a crossroads. A dozen identical strings tied into one giant, impossible knot. A dozen identical strings leading to a dozen different destinations on the property. I stood there with the original string in my hand, deciding which string to follow. I squatted in the dirt, my knees pushing my white nightgown into the earth as I attempted to detangle the mess of possible outcomes and pick the right path.

Enzo stood over me and said, "You sure that's the right string?"

"Well, now I'm not!"

I held the knot in my hand and chose a path. The string led me down the forested hill to the shore. It traced the tide, anchored with seashells and softened green glass, then led back up toward the house. Enzo towered over me and said, "Keep going."

I followed the string back up, to the out-of-commission boat beside the house. The boat in which I would sit and pretend to be a pirate some days, pretend to be a princess other days. The string disappeared into a hole in the side of the boat and reappeared on the other side. It led me around the back of the house and slipped under the door to the basement, the door I was very much afraid to open.

"Open it," Enzo said.

I took a deep breath and opened the paint-chipped door. The string disappeared down the staircase into the dark basement below. I squeezed my palm shut, wishing the string was thick enough to push back against my hand, then began walking down the stairs.

The steps creaked like an old witch stretching, and that was definitely a rat I just heard as I shuffled my boots along the floor. The string circled around a pillar in the middle of the room, then disappeared once again, under a door in the corner. A door I was sure hadn't been there a second before.

"Open the door, Hayley," Enzo whispered.

I reached out my hand and turned the knob. Sitting on a chair with the string tied to her wrist was a tiny porcelain girl. She was wearing a long, poofy dress and her hair was curly but had dirt and bits of kindling in it, like she'd had to fight to get to that chair. And I knew her right away. I burst forward and untied the string from her wrist, pulling her to my chest and calling her by name.

"Sara!"

Over the previous few weeks, Enzo had told me all about her. In bedtime story installments, he told me about this girl not unlike me, who was captured by an evil family. About how she escaped only to be scooped up by an angry eagle, which then carried her to its nest, where it planned to raise her as its own. He told me how she tricked the eagle to leave the nest one afternoon and slid down the side of the tree to run through the fields in search of shelter with a leaf pressed tightly to her head, ensuring the eagle would mistake her for just a bit of green on the breeze. He described her in perfect detail. Her auburn hair and white dress and how lucky she would be to find me.

"Sara, Sara, Sara!" I kissed her face and felt her tiny porcelain arms rest on my shoulders. I carried her out of the basement.

Now, with someone to protect, it didn't seem so scary. I had someone to be brave for.

"Thank you, Enzo." Sara and I ran at him, wrapping our bodies around his leg.

So, this was Enzo, my hero.

But this was also Enzo: My family was watching TV in the living room one afternoon when Enzo was in town visiting. I got up to go to the bathroom. I sat down on the toilet and started peeing.

In a second my pants were soaked, and I didn't understand why. The floor was flooding and I didn't get it and I couldn't figure out why I was sitting in a bowl of my own piss all of a sudden. I couldn't understand why it wasn't going into the toilet like it should be.

I stood up and looked behind me, where I made out the barely reflective surface of a sheet of cellophane tightly secured over the toilet bowl. I was eight.

As I opened the door and yelled for my mother, I heard Enzo start to laugh. He laughed uncontrollably, cackling at my embarrassment. Enjoying my shame.

And I loved him.

And it's only now that I see what happens when you love someone who makes you feel immeasurable joy and impossible pain in equal measure. It's only now that I see how that has manifested in my adult life, how quickly and carelessly I discount extraordinary pain for someone I deem magical, for someone who makes me special by proximity.

So now I have to kill you, too, Enzo.

I have to lose you to love me.

tal

his voice and her face

I've watched this video dozens of times. Its only thirty seconds long. Its thumbnail is an out-of-focus shot of a girl's face. Her bright-pink nails are pressed against her lips and her eyes are closed.

I know she is me, because I remember when she bought that dress at Goodwill and I remember that particular cat eye she did for almost a full year when she was living in the house with the man-boys. Her cheeks are flushed as she sheepishly attempts to respond to a voice we can hear from somewhere else in the barely lit room.

This video is a self-portrait of my fumbling inability to stand up for myself with Tal. As I watch, I strain to hear the specific words his furious voice is yelling at my stunned expression, my subservient gaze.

If my computer camera had been rolling earlier, we would have seen me in the busy living room, holding a hand of cards at a flimsy poker table.

We would have seen me win.

We would have watched my arms reach out and collect the pile of plastic chips. Then we would have seen playful Tal transform into a billowing black cloud. We would have watched him stand up in front of a room of men and start screaming at me.

He was sure I'd cheated. I hadn't.

We'd see a room of men cowardly attempt to calm him down, and then, quickly giving up, grab their valuables and decidedly run into their underground bunkers to seek safety from the storm. Perhaps mostly afraid of losing their meal tickets if they stood up too aggressively for me.

I tried, in tiny bursts of confidence, to assure him that I hadn't cheated. He barely let me speak, so eventually I walked out of the room to sit on my bed and turn on Photo Booth, hoping to capture my empty, broken expression. Hoping that eventually, watching enough of this collected proof would gain me the courage to lock him out of my life forever.

Now, on camera, he screams as I begin shrinking. Everything about me getting smaller and smaller. As I watch I wonder, if he hadn't walked out of the room, would I have disappeared altogether? Shrinking and shrinking to the sound of hair catching on fire, eventually leaving just a tiny red pile of ash on the keyboard of my computer?

We see me in the frame, listening and listening, then speaking up. He does not stop yelling.

"Are you gonna let me say anything?" I ask, making eye contact with him for the first time.

"No," he barks.

We can hear him mumble something. He storms out of the room, slamming the door behind him. My hand reaches up and covers my face, then the video stops.

mom

what i talk about when i talk about lemons

My dad stood in our kitchen, holding three lemons. He was supposed to pick up eight.

My mom exploded at him as my sisters and I watched him fail to defend himself, standing with his red nose and snowy boots in a puddle of water by the back door. He'd misheard. He thought she'd said three. He held the insufficient lemons in his hands, staring into their joyful yellow faces, as if willing them to multiply.

I was fifteen. In an attempt to defend him, I looked up from the homework I was pretending to do and said, "Mom, he thought it was three. It's not a big deal."

She got furious and I couldn't understand her fury. It was five missing lemons. What could possibly be so upsetting about five missing lemons?

It's only now that I notice the moulding lemon in the bowl on my counter and realize the effect those five missing lemons have had on my life, the big, rotting lemon seed they planted in me. A lemon seed that has been secretly nurturing my belief that a woman who is expressing anger is ugly and a man who is apologetic is sad.

And so I have refused to be angry and I have sought out men who never apologize for anything.

Of course this lesson didn't come from lemons alone. This lesson came from years of exchanges like this one, exchanges that, fifteen years after the fact, made me analyze why I have never fully expressed my anger to any man.

And suddenly I want to pull a *High Fidelity*–style cleaning of my slate by calling every ex-lover to be honest about how I felt, a decade later in some cases. To finally accept Joe Schmo's persistent LinkedIn request only to tell him that the thing he did eight years ago was really fucking bullshit. To go back in time and relive my life without the belief that to be an angry woman is ugly, now that I realize how different my life would look with that single lens adjustment.

My mom had been in the kitchen cooking for at least six hours. My siblings and I watched her gracefully float around the room, mixing sauces and dipping her bare pointer finger into a pot of boiling water before dropping the artichokes into the scalding steam. We sat at the dining room table offering her no assistance, then complaining when she asked us for anything. We complained before the ask, even. She was like those people on Hyperion Avenue who want you to sign up to save all the puppies in the world or give an entire village medical care for five dollars a year. We ignored her before she could even extend her clipboard. She could have been offering us a no-strings-attached trip to Disney World and we wouldn't have realized it. We'd have been well into the chip aisle in Trader Joe's before she got to her pitch.

"Excuse me, do you have a second to save the entire human race from extinction in exchange for a signature?"

"No, sorry, no time. Must get plantain chips. Fuck you."

My dad stood in our kitchen holding three lemons. He was supposed to pick up eight.

My mom got furious and now I get it. She was furious because those lemons were not just lemons. Those lemons were a symbol of her exhaustion, because she worked full-time and parented full-time while my dad toured, and she loved him, and she missed him, and she felt alone, and she just needed eight lemons.

My dad thought it was three because he just did. He thought it was three because people mishear and forget and if you put a *3* against a mirror, it looks like an *8*. He'd been pulled away from his family for a blossoming career, and when he was home, he was our hero because we missed him. And that wasn't his fault, but it wasn't my mom's fault, either. It's just what happened.

And now maybe I can see the beauty and purpose in my mother's anger and that will make room for my own.

And maybe now I can see the beauty and importance in my dad's fragility and that will make room for a different kind of man in my life.

diego

before we were friends

I inherited a piano when a friend's mom died unexpectedly and their family had to quickly find a home for the gorgeous old upright. It's black and spent most of my Silver Lake life tucked in the corner of my room by a small wooden window that refused to open. I covered it with plants in various stages of dying. There was a little pink bundle murdered by my fingers earlier that morning when I tore it from its family on my walk. There was a small bouquet of dried roses spray-painted vibrant metallic blue from when some friends shot a music video in my room almost six months before.

Just over the ivory keys, Joni Mitchell's self-portrait stared out at me from the front of her 1969 *Clouds* LP cover. Right above Joni sat a long piece of dried cholla cactus, covered in tiny little holes that would have been a major issue for my sister and her trypophobia. Except for that morning's dead pink bundle, this piece of cactus was the newest addition to my bedroom/museum of rotting things. I had picked it up during a four-day trip to Death Valley a week earlier. The surprisingly wonderful trip to Death Valley with Paul and Diego and Marc.

I met Marc and Diego when I was sixteen, while visiting Paul at school in Montreal. They were classmates, and I have been dazzled and in some kind of love with all of them at several points in my life. They all randomly and independently moved to L.A. during my first two years there, and had I been able to see even a foot outside my tiny Tal bubble, they would have been an incredible support system for me.

It was just after 8:00 p.m. I'd been hiding in my room, and it smelled like a fortune teller's den. I'd burned mounds of palo santo and sage and cedar. The room was musky and dark and cold, and I refused to turn on any lights. I bundled myself up in layers of Goodwill sweaters and remembered that it was autumn somewhere.

I could hear Diego in the hall. If I were to just rotate on my piano chair, I'd be able to see him, too. I'd see his silhouette through the nearly opaque curtains hanging over my fully glass doors. The doors connecting my room to the living room.

I was hiding because I was embarrassed.

I was hiding because, after nine years of not seeing each other and barely speaking, we went on this kind of perfect desert trip where I got to be who I really am. I got to show him and, more importantly, myself that I could eat fries now. I could drink and disagree with him. I was expressive and funny and vulnerable and present.

Sitting in the back seat of my Honda Fit, inches away from him, I could step out from behind all of my bullshit insecurities long enough to actually get to know him for a minute. And suddenly it felt like we were friends. Like we had a real shot at a real friendship, and so ...

I tried to fuck him two days after we got back.

I'd sent him a very direct, let-me-come-meet-you-somewhere proposition in email form. I wiped my emotional muscle memory clean and dove right back down to where our relationship had started nine years before, behind the safety of a computer screen.

And I'd put effort into it. I had curled up in my bed to run the combinations of words through my internal processing system in the hopes of stumbling across some sentence that would make him say yes. Almost negotiating with him. Though not him, really. I'd typed alone in my bed, outlining how little it had to mean. Explaining how casual and string-free it could be. How good I was at not letting myself feel the things I was feeling now. How impressed he'd be with how insignificant I could make sex now.

And I thought he was going to say yes and all my pain surrounding him would suddenly end. We'd tuck it into some bed along the Pacific Coast Highway and all my pain would suddenly make sense, all my endurance would finally have a finish line.

He sent me this simple reply: "Hayley. No. We'll talk when I'm back in a couple days." Now he was staying in our guest room, for one last night, while I waited in dread for the impending conversation.

And I thought, *Maybe if I step on the mute pedal, I can play quietly without him hearing me. Or maybe I shouldn't risk it. Maybe I can just sit silently until he's gone.*

Maybe if I'm still enough he won't notice the quietly flickering candles perched on my piano. Or maybe I should just blow them out.

Maybe he doesn't smell the freshly lit cedar seeping out from under my door. Maybe he can't feel the space I'm taking up.

I know I won't be that lucky, though. I know he's gonna knock. I can feel him inching toward my door, pulling his fingers into his palm to make a fist. I can feel him lifting his hand to knock on the glass.

He knocked.

I said, "Come in," but not because I wanted him to. He opened the door and the living room light flooded into my dungeon, aggressively backlighting him as he stood still in my doorway as if he were waiting for another invitation. I looked over my shoulder and smiled apologetically at him. I smiled like a puppy sheepishly standing over a mound of chewed-up leather that used to be your favourite shoe.

If we had to have this conversation, I was glad it was going to happen in my smoky little dungeon, with me sitting at that piano. It was probably the only place in the world where I felt like I had the upper hand. Getting rejected or reliving past rejection felt easier to handle in front of something that could never reject me.

And something that would never love him the way it loved me.

Music will never give to him the same way it gives to me. It will never work through him the way it works through me, and that made me feel big and safe and ready.

He closed the door behind him. Crawling into the darkness to sit beside me on the chair I got from the Rose Bowl Flea Market a few weeks before.

He was about to launch into it. I sat still and nervous and barely making eye contact with him.

And suddenly it was like nine years hadn't gone by. Like I was back in Paris. And I started thinking, *Maybe I should go run him a shower. Tell him he doesn't have to do this. Tell him I'll understand if he wants to go hide in the bathroom and pretend I don't exist.*

I looked back to my keys to play a D minor triad. It's a very sad chord, but it stabilized me. Reminding me I could have a secret conversation with this instrument while he rejected me again. I could be loved by this piano while he told me again that he couldn't love me.

He inhaled, slowly, deliberately, his tongue pressing against his imperfect bottom teeth as he prepared to speak. "That trip happened. We did that. All those flights and trains and hostels. All those letters and plans. Those were real. But everything that happened after was real, too. And you have to stop inviting people who have hurt you back into your heart and bed. I lost that privilege. If I was even a slightly less good guy it would be so easy to take advantage of you. And I really love you, Hayley."

I listened and cried. He cried, too.

And suddenly it felt like a gift. Like someone's head had been blocking the sun and all he needed to do was lean down to pick something up off the floor and I'd be blinded by the yellow light.

I could see that by him saying no, I was freed.

When I am not trying to get something from someone, when I'm not trying to shape myself into something I think might suit someone, I make space to feel everything I've been trying not to feel. When I remove motive, I make space to be angry and hurt. I make space to miss him. I make space to love him. I make space to forgive him.

And in doing that I make space to miss and love and forgive myself.

And suddenly I didn't feel like it was nine years ago again. I felt like it was a week ago again. I felt like we were back in my Honda Fit driving home from Death Valley.

Like we're laughing as I show him how to make a very bad beat using GarageBand on my iPad. Like we're wedging our knees against the backs of the seats in front of us and quietly rolling our eyes at each other while Marc and Paul bicker about something. Marc winning, of course, because Marc always wins.

Paul folding like a cheap beach chair, its metal frame jutting out from under its thin fabric.

Like Diego is picking on me for something I said. But it isn't cruel. It's funny and I can't stop laughing. The woven seats are covered in sand from our shoes and shirts and pockets. There's a half-full bag of Marc's homemade caramel popcorn on the floor. I reach for it because the thought of Diego seeing me eat doesn't kill me anymore.

Like "The Only Living Boy in New York" is playing off my iPod, making me feel like Natalie Portman in *Garden State*. I am pressing my face against the window, watching the giant golden sand dunes speed by, becoming one seamless giant golden sand dune.

Like I turn and see him with his headphones on, adding a synthetic guitar riff to the beat he's making on my iPad. I know it can't possibly be good, and that makes me happy. He's chewing on his bottom lip and bobbing his head to the beat. He looks six years old now. I look six years old, too.

Like we might have a real shot at a real friendship.

I reached out to play the crisp, clean, out-of-tune middle C on my piano and it brought me back to the moment.

I let his words wash over me as I started to play something on the keys. An improvised melody that completely captured how I was feeling. It perfectly expressed this beautiful letting go. It perfectly captured my vulnerability and the start of something new.

And suddenly I felt understood and I felt caught and I felt seen.

I turned to him to speak. I pressed my tongue against the back of my teeth and said, out loud, "Thank you."

paul

what we're not saying

After our desert trip, Diego, Paul, and I basically only brush against each other's lives in Marc-adjacent events. And when we are together, it slams me down in my life like I'm a narrator. Like I'm writing my life as it happens, in real time. Like this:

I am sitting alone on Marc's front porch, looking out at his new and extraordinary garden, this wild and unusual combination of plants that could coexist only in Los Angeles. It isn't pretty; it is impressive and relentless and a yard-sized display of his obsessive genius.

It's his birthday and one of the few times Diego, Paul, and I are all in the same room since our trip three years earlier. There's a little clump of balloons floating over my head as I listen to the blossoming party inside, the clanking of the things and the simmering of the stuff and the yelling of the Marc.

I guess I tried to look pretty today. I blow-dried and curled my hair and put on a little bit more makeup than I usually do. I bought paper nipple covers at CVS on the way to the party and slipped them over my braless tits at a red light a few blocks away.

I'm sitting outside, quietly collecting myself. Though, not myself, really — I'm kind of getting into character. I'm shifting in my dress, a dress I chose specifically because it's a combination of comfortable and uncomfortable. It has one busted sliding strap and a casually plunging neckline, ensuring that I will never get fully relaxed for the duration of the party. It will ever-so-subtly force me to sit up a bit straighter, pull my stomach in a bit tighter, laugh a bit differently. It will calmly encourage me to keep my involuntary act perfectly in place.

I'm sure Paul is going to arrive in a minute, and I will say hi and he will say hi and we will pretend that we are strangers, kind of. Strangers who knew each other a bit, a while ago.

We will not discuss our ten years of friendship. We will not share stories or laugh about shared memories. I will not say anything that starts with *Oh fuck, remember when* … This is the agreement we have silently, invisibly, secretly made independently of each other. The agreement to not remember out loud. Perhaps to not remember at all.

We will hug for a split second. Our bodies will be stiff and cold, and we will quickly look somewhere else as we pull away to ensure our eyes don't meet when we are close enough to lick each other's cheeks or lips or noses.

I just saw them walking up to the house, Paul and his wife. Her flowing black hair reflected in my car window as they passed

the front gate. He's walking like he does onstage. He's performing, too. He's in character, too. Just like me. Our characters are
strangers, kind of. We are strangers who knew each other a bit, a
while ago.

I'm staying seated out here because that way we'll only have
to have a quick, casual greeting on the porch before they walk
inside to find the birthday boy. It will be totally kind and a bit
funny and we will both intentionally keep it very short. We will
be a barista and a customer who realize they are from the same
small town and have an unexpectedly playful rapport.

He's a bit tanned and a bit uncomfortable in his own skin.
He's like that sugar-water alien at the beginning of *Men in Black*.
I imagine he's like this only when he's uncomfortable. Adjusting
his suit of human skin over his alien body, trying very hard to
seem chill and easygoing and relaxed.

I'm going to go inside in a minute. I'm praying Paul and his
wife don't ask me about my music. I desperately don't want to
fill them in on my career. I don't want them to nod in unison
and congratulate me for anything at all. Their Pleasantville smiles
on their somehow connected faces grinning as they tell me how
great I'm doing.

I take a plate from Marc's outstretched hand. I am having a
piece of birthday pie. It's full of calories and fat and gluten, and I
am going to eat it with a casual smile and quietly feel like I'm better than Paul's wife, who has decided to nibble from Paul's plate.
I will feel proud of my ability to add *carefree eater* to the list of
characteristics this totally fake performative version of myself has.

Paul and I are careful not to make eye contact, ensuring we
are not hurled into a sort of time warp. We are careful to avoid
any lingering anything to ensure we do not revisit any snapshot
of our past.

I will leave the room when the conversation seems to be
drifting in my direction.

I will actively avoid looking at his fingers, remembering the years of letters.

I will avoid his mouth, dodging the memories of him going down on me for the first time on the dock at my cabin when I was sixteen.

I will avoid the back of his neck, knowing how the short bristles of hair felt against my palm as he threw up into the kitchen sink at Victoria Beach.

I will avoid his feet and my secret knowledge of his nailless toes.

I will avoid his jokes, ensuring that I don't laugh at something nobody else seems to find funny, accidently exposing our natural chemistry.

I will avoid his boxy hands and the years of clutching beer bottles in Winnipeg basements.

I will avoid his smiles and suggestions and ideas and words and the decade of trips and meals and canoes and exploration.

I will avoid eating anything that tastes bitter while looking at him, quietly reminded of how his cum tasted in the back seat of my parents' minivan.

I will pretend I don't know how much he likes my ass, and I will try to walk to the bathroom with my hands clasped behind my back, but as normally as possible.

I will avoid him by avoiding me.

"Wow, we have three people here from Winnipeg," Marc says as he walks into the dining room, opening a bottle of wine.

This comment makes me instantly angry. Marc is breaking the rules. Marc is referencing a past that Paul and I share. Marc is referencing a shared history that we must actively avoid to keep this show moving smoothly.

But I wonder what would happen if I jumped into this shimmering, gelatinous blob he just released into the room. I wonder what would happen if I could stand up and grab the glistening metallic orb and pull it around Paul and me like a force field. If we could step into this humming in-between and freeze everyone else into a party tableau, impossibly still, midconversation, midbite, middrink, midlaugh. The flickering flames coming to a full, terrifying stop.

And we would notice we were the only ones still animated. And I would walk over to him with my hand extended and say, "Hi, Paul. Remember me?"

And he would smile and exhale at the same time and reply, "Hi, Hayley. I remember you. Do you remember me?"

And I think we would laugh and walk around the room and poke at people's frozen faces. I would dare him to dip Marc's mom's finger into a tub of butter and he would do it, then laugh and get so embarrassed and turn so red and wipe it off with a tea towel. Then we would go outside and do cartwheels between the plants. Paul would tip over some potted thing and we would prop it back up together while his eyes disappeared behind his squinty laugh.

And we wouldn't fuck or kiss, even. We would just play. I would hit a note on the piano and make him try to match it with his voice. He would fail and we would laugh until we cried. We would talk about our teenage improv troop and years of shows and costumes and family dinners. I would describe his family home in detail and he would describe mine. We would, for a moment, share witness to each other's childhoods.

Then I would say, "I found this box of letters from you. Years of letters. Letters with photos and drawings and CDs attached. I think I forgot that we really loved each other. And I am furious that you don't know how to make platonic space for someone you loved once. I am sad that you have to avoid your life to live with yourself."

And I think maybe he would understand what I mean.

"Wow, we have three people here from Winnipeg," Marc says as he walks into the dining room, opening a bottle of wine.

This comment makes me instantly angry. Marc is breaking the rules.

I grab my wine glass and begin walking toward the bathroom as I say over my shoulder, "Oh my god, that's right. I always forget that you're from Winnipeg too, Robbie!"

I slip into the bathroom and spritz myself with Marc's expensive cologne and plunge a Q-tip into my ear, letting my eyes roll back into my head as I sit on the edge of the tub for a minute, then flush the empty toilet and come back out into the party.

"Fuck, guys, I'm wiped. I'm gonna go home."

And I am really exhausted. I'm exhausted from not being myself, and I'm realizing I don't want to do this anymore. I don't want to be anywhere that I can't be myself.

I'm realizing that even though this was in every way a fun, relaxed, conflict-free night, I don't want to be around Paul anymore.

I don't want to avoid my life to live with myself, and I don't want to help him do it either.

mom

patterns

It's a beautiful and equally devastating thing to realize your parents are just people. Your mom is her mom's daughter. Your dad is his dad's son, and everything you are is because of everything they did. And everything they did is because of everything their parents did and their parents' parents and so on and so forth, so far back until there is nothing but infinite space and impossible blackness and unimaginable quiet.

It was Christmas Eve. We were at my mom's house. Kendra and I sat facing each other at the corner of the table, giggling in a way that only sisters do, as our mother disappeared into a cloud of steam in the kitchen, then emerged from it with a platter of crab legs. Darrell was on the other end of the table. Darrell, my mother's on-again, off-again partner since my parents' divorce. It was a very civilized scene. Darrell drank from his shaken vodka martini as my mother, in a baby-blue apron, laid the platter on the table. Kendra and I continued to counteract the civility by regressing into our teenage selves, deliberately slouching, intentionally enjoying private inside jokes without even the offer of guiding breadcrumbs.

Christmas Eve did not look like this growing up. My three siblings and I would scarf down dinner, eating like we were speeding through traffic, barely paying attention to the red lights and street signs, tiny deadly salmon bones and unwanted greens. My father would play his Christmas album and my mom would whisper, "Did you check under the tree? I wonder if Santa left something tonight."

We would abandon the candlelit table and run into the living room, where we would, year after year, find a flawless, Martha Stewartesque moment. The fireplace would be crackling behind a giant glowing tree drenched in years of ornaments, each connected with some specific, deeply significant event, memory, or person. The corners of the room would be softened by the scalloped lines of drooping, sparkling Christmas lights, and my clinically obese cat would push his flabby body into the scattered pine needles and wedge himself between four perfectly wrapped gifts.

Our family felt perfect to me. It felt perfect because it was meant to. It felt perfect because my mother made the decision to create for us the childhood she never had. My parents decided to create for us the childhoods neither of them had. We were gifted this deliberately unblemished, candy-coated, gift-wrapped youth. A type of perfection that takes time to recover from, actually, because inevitably, any chapter that follows one called "Perfect" is going to be called "Oh Wait, What?" or "Realizing Perfect Isn't a Real Thing."

Darrell moved on to wine. He cracked a bottle of white as Kendra and I swigged back the last of the gin from our spotless crystal glasses. This year, the guest list for this Christmas Eve dinner table had been trimmed down significantly. My sister Danica now had a gorgeous little girl and my brother had two incredible sons. My dad had an extraordinary new wife and they were all creating new patterns and new traditions.

And there we were, Darrell, Mom, Kendra, and me. This Christmas boiled down to the four of us as a result of ten thousand dollars. Ten thousand teeny, tiny, little dollars that were meant to be our inheritance from our grandfather. Without getting into every move and email and conversation, let me offer you the Coles Notes version so we all have the same information moving forward:

1. Our grandpa is ninety-eight, so, like any second now …
2. He was planning to leave the grandkids, of which I am one, a total of ten thousand dollars.
3. It has been revealed, to no one's surprise, that he likes my uncle's son, Brady, most of all because Brady plays tennis — and I guess he likes tennis. Therefore, he believes Brady should get the full ten grand.
4. This choosing of a favourite grandchild has let loose decades of sibling and family drama on my mom's side, including a number of emails that feature phrases like *You're dead to me*, as well as a few inappropriate phone calls to my sisters and brother, attempting to convince them that our mother is a terrible person.

Yes, there is significantly more nuance to it than that, but it's boring. I'm bored. Bottom line, when someone picks a favourite, years of resentment and abuse and shit gets shaken out of the past like pebbles out of an upside-down shoe. What is important for you to know is that my mother has been incredibly close to her brothers all her life. Growing up, her older brother, Enzo, was her lifeline in an unstable home. At one time, she felt for her brothers the way I feel for my siblings, cloaked in an entirely unshakable love and bond. I can't even imagine a scenario in which my siblings and I would feel even slightly less in love with each other.

Needless to say, my mother's heart had been broken and it was devastating to watch. The decision to spend this Christmas without her brothers had been brutally hard for us to make as a family.

At the dinner table, we were just talking about olives. Like, how good they are and how psychotic it is to put unpitted olives in a martini. To wedge a toothpick along one side of the pit so it's all uncentred, barely holding on to the insufficient amount of olive flesh you've given it to dangle from.

Then Darrell's quiet expression turned busy and turbulent as he took a sip of his chardonnay. He looked at me and said, "I don't know what your issue is with your mom's family, but if you don't see them tomorrow, you'll regret it forever."

The room instantly became ten degrees hotter. I took a deep breath and said, "Sorry, I just need a second to figure out how to respond to that kindly."

Darrell leaned back in his chair and casually spit, "Why? Go for it," and suddenly I saw the three lemons in my dad's outstretched hand, and I realized I had access to my anger. I realized I could see how to uncouple anger from meanness. I realized my anger had purpose and value.

"Our decision to spend tomorrow without my uncles and Nonna was made with great care," I started. "We spoke to a therapist and spent hours discussing how abusive the last couple years have been. We did not passively come to this decision."

Fully yelling now, my whole body shaking as I hovered off my chair in a rage-filled glute exercise that would make any personal trainer proud, I continued. "You have been in and out of our lives for the last two years, and what would be awesome is for you to just support the decision my mother has made. A decision that was really, really hard for her to make. A decision that we made as a family to no longer normalize the abuse she has endured. That says you can't treat a person like shit on Tuesday, then take them out for dinner on Wednesday. Or even worse, expect them to cook *you* dinner on Wednesday. You're not a wizard, Darrell. You don't know what's gonna happen down the line. And maybe instead of casting this black-cloud prophecy of future regret over my mother's head, you support the decision she has made and help her negotiate her future pain as it actually happens."

The tablecloth bubbled out from between my scrunched fingers as I stood up, my skin on fire, shaking like a set of fresh-from-the-tub, chattering teeth. "I actually can't stay at this table right now," I said.

Darrell was emasculated. He didn't know how to respond. He looked small. He looked like a bully who'd started picking on me when we were both sitting and didn't realize I was twice his size until I stood up. He folded his arms against his chest. "Hayley. You're always so fucking dramatic."

And just like that, I was done. Just like that, in six words and one breath, he took one tiny step that just happened to be over the edge of a building. He took one tiny step that was impossible to come back from. And this comment was particularly hurtful, of course, because it's true. I am dramatic, but I love that I am. I love that I am passionate about things that matter in my life. I love that heartbreaks debilitate me for weeks, months, years. I love that I feel like I'm in a movie every time I jog. I love that I usually open my eyes and scream when my head is fully submerged in a bathtub.

My mother's face became so deeply sad, this very particular shade of purple. A bit blue from knowing how right I was, a bit red in a reflection of my bloodshot cheeks, and a bit white out of embarrassment and fear and the realization that this moment would be pivotal.

I walked away from the table with Kendra at my side. We hid in my mom's den. It's this cozy room where I can see more of my mother's personality. Her jewellery is draped over the outstretched arms of a little metal tree in the corner. Pieces of her homemade stained glass hang down over the windows, frozen pink and blue and orange fireflies and hummingbirds waiting for the sun to stream through them, faintly covering the room with tiny pools of coloured light. Kendra and I sat on the brown fold-out couch under a photograph of my niece and nephews. I could hear my mother talking to Darrell in the other room as my anger became empathetic devastation and my face turned the same shade of purple my mother's had just worn.

As if in a significantly less fun *Freaky Friday*, a perfect bolt of lightning struck the stained-glass hummingbird on the window and the house shook, and I blinked and my mother blinked and suddenly I was her and she was her mother. I was her tiny eight-year-old body, hiding in this back room because I felt unsafe. I was hiding back here because the world is huge and I felt alone in it. And my mother was her mother, in the living room talking down the man she loved. She was putting her foot down while trying to figure out a way to continue loving him and loving us at the same time.

And I think, maybe, the question is not whether we become like our parents — because of course we do. The question is this: What version of our parents do we become? At what stage in their development do we stop and pitch a tent? Do we become the person they were as children or in high school? Maybe we settle into their personalities as husbands or wives. Maybe we become the optimistic people they were as first-time parents or settle into their fractured selves as divorcees.

Maybe the question is not whether we become like our parents. Rather, can we notice which version we've become and find a way to sympathize with them based on that self-reflection?

mom

christ is born, hallelujah

It was 5:00 p.m. Darrell would be back for dinner any minute. I guess he'd spent the afternoon hiding in some 7-Eleven or seeing a movie or going for Chinese food or something.

Kendra and I had spent the morning being waited on by my mother because she felt horrible. She brought us breakfast and coffee in bed after I made it blatantly clear that I would not be sitting at the breakfast table with Darrell to compassionately receive his apology and pave the way for a more resilient relationship.

Now it was time for dinner. "Okay, everyone to the table!" my mother declared excitedly.

Darrell came in through the back door and I began my performance as a person who was totally okay with this situation, a role I knew how to play very well. I sat at the head of the table, my dad on the other end, which I would normally love. We would normally shoot each other playful, knowing looks throughout the meal and sweetly roll our eyes at the same things and laugh at the same jokes. But tonight he sat beside Darrell and he didn't yet know about our Christmas Eve. He didn't know because I very deliberately withheld that information from him and everyone else at this table who hadn't been there the night before. I thought it better to let them live outside the conflict, at least until Darrell wasn't at the receiving end of a chicken leg or the bowl of roasted carrots or a carving knife.

I was doing exactly what my mother had done for as many of my teenage years as she could, until she just couldn't anymore. My mother hid her unhappiness until it reached a boiling point, until that boiling point triggered one tiny step that just happened to be over the edge of a building and she free-fell into becoming consumed by her legitimate pain and anger.

Hiding true feelings for long periods of time robs you of your chance to put your pain and trauma in the right place. Then, all of a sudden, it's ten years later and you're furious about three missing lemons, when it's not at all about lemons.

And here I was, doing exactly what I had been silently taught how to do, compartmentalizing and hiding challenging information to protect the people around me.

I'd arranged the seating plan before Darrell arrived so I could predetermine my sightlines for the evening, therefore assuring I would absolutely avoid any unexpected eye contact. I put my sisters on either side of me, like two life rafts that I could reach out to and grab in a moment, should things get rocky.

I looked around the table at all my loved ones in their sweet obliviousness and realized that it was in no way shocking that I'd ended up the other woman in an affair for almost six years.

For so much of my life, I was on the outside of significant information. Painful truths were withheld from me, for reasonable reasons. And waking up from that perfection was very hard for me. Realizing the world isn't this perfect place where everything you want magically rolls down a red carpet for you was hard for me. Realizing that people you love can lie to you was hard for me.

So when my relationship with Tal evolved into a web of secrets and private, unspeakable betrayals, I felt safe in it. I felt safe in it because I wasn't outside it. I felt safe in it because at least I got to have all the information. Out of all the women in his life, at least I knew him for real. At least I could pride myself on being the woman who accepted him for exactly who he was, even at my own expense.

Like, the only thing worse than being on the inside would be being on the outside. The only thing worse than being one of his many women on the side would be not knowing you were one.

Molly used to come visit Tal before she fully moved to L.A. By the time we were deep into it, he made sure I wasn't around for these visits, just in case my mood ring of a face gave away the entire operation. I would sit at a friend's place and pace and not eat and love my disappearing trauma body. I would obsessively check my calendar, waiting for the day circled in red, the day when she would be leaving. And I would hate myself. I would hate how easy it had become to keep secrets, how good I was getting at lying, how far I was moving away from who I thought I was. But the only person I was more terrified of being was Molly. I am sure there are affairs where the other woman wishes she wasn't just that, but that wasn't me. I was terrified of being the woman with a man lying to her twenty-four hours a day, 365 days a year. I was terrified of waking up one morning to realize that everything I thought to be true had been a lie.

lander

i was thirty-one; he wasn't

Like Edward Scissorhands without the scissors, he walked up to me and said, "Hi. I'm Lander."

I said, "Oh, wow, I really like your face."

He laughed. "I really like your face."

In a black button-up and dress pants, he shyly hugged me, then profusely apologized for the café and the shitty comedian and the vibe and said maybe he should have picked a different place, somewhere else.

He ordered us two green-tea smoothies. We sat down out-side at a little patio table. I asked him where he lived.

This line of questioning exposed the first clue that I should perhaps confirm how old he was.

He didn't share a house with three other guys; he shared a room with three other guys. Imagining yourself at thirty-one stepping over unconscious dudes is a very effective form of contraception. I was finally a few years past my time in the man-boy abode, living with six guys. I was finally living in a place of my own, so, like, no more tiny, mysterious black hairs in my sink. Thanks.

"Wait, how old are you?"

"Um, I'm young, you know, but age is just a number.... I'm nineteen," he said.

I laughed, realizing this date was going to be less a date and more a guidance counsellor meeting. He was a violinist at UCLA. A charming, sensitive, ambitious, emotionally articulate violinist at UCLA.

He earnestly asked me about my experiences in the music industry, how to get a publishing deal, what it looks like when you do get one. Listening intently to every word out of my mouth, not once interacting with his phone.

At nine thirty the café servers started coming outside to pull down the umbrellas and clear the tables. Realizing we were getting the boot, we got up and I asked him if he needed a ride. He said he didn't.

I walked him to a baby-blue bicycle with a large black basket for books and groceries and his violin. Lingering on this quiet street corner, I thought, *I can't make a move on this guy.*

I barely got to the end of the thought before he leaned in and kissed me, a sweet sincere kiss, the bike still wedged between us. I put one hand on his chest, feeling his heart pound, remem-bering my own heart pounding out of my chest when I kissed

Diego for the first time, when I was nineteen. Remembering the fear and excitement and nervousness.

After a few minutes, we stopped and giggled at each other. We kissed one more time in front of my car.

After one last tender hug, I drove away and never saw him again.

len

time for a test

Every partner has taught me something. Even the shitty ones. Maybe even more so the shitty ones. The ones I've sacrificed my integrity for. The ones I've blindly put my body in danger for. The ones I've lied to about being on birth control, then secretly taken dozens of morning-after pills for. The ones I've gotten piercings for. The ones I've skipped dinners to do laundry for. The ones I've cooked and cleaned and waxed for.

The ones I've helped maintain multiple secret relationships.

The ones whose sexual preferences I've claimed were mine, too. Whose morning rituals I've adopted. Whose entire personalities I have latched on to. Not necessarily making myself just like them, but making myself into exactly what I've felt they needed. The perfect counterpart. Not a total yes-man, but sparing and defiant with my noes. Expertly scattering them over a series of hangouts to appear easygoing and chill, yet sure of myself.

Len and I met at a studio at the top of a winding hill ten minutes from my new apartment in Los Feliz. The apartment that turned my growth and sense of self-worth into a pinpoint on a map.

I could not have created a more stunningly packaged weakness for myself. He was like a perfectly Frankensteined version of all the men I have loved in my life. This tall, dark, flopsy-haired musician with huge hands, which I would later tell him were beloved by all women because he was basically walking around with two hands of cock fingers.

Five cocks per hand. Eleven cocks total.

I could almost smell his feelings for me, like a Solo cup of abandoned beer leaning against the leg of a picnic table on a sickeningly hot summer day.

He walked me out after our writing session ended. We lingered in front of our cars while he listed restaurants in my new neighbourhood that I hadn't been to. It's kind of a genius technique actually: "You've never been to Fred 62? Oh my god, I'll take you." Before you know it, you have casually scheduled a date without having to be asked or having to say yes. Genius.

He picked Fred 62 because it was close to my place. I liked that. We giggled at each other across the neon-green patio table under the yellow-tinted lights as he casually took my left hand in his. I turned my head in the hopes that he wouldn't notice the unmistakable wave of blood rushing to my face.

One of the issues with wearing my new favourite all-white outfit was that it highlighted my debilitating blushing disorder.

While no doctor has ever told me I have a blushing disorder, doctors miss things all the time. As sure as the sun will rise, so will my face turn red. Impossible-to-ignore, bright, throbbing red, and when it's at the top of an all-white moment, I might as well be a cherry lollipop. That bright, sweet, obvious red orb with its long white cardboard stick that shreds apart in your hand at the slightest hint of moisture.

By 3:00 a.m., we were nearly five hours past my bedtime. "Fuck, I'm keeping you out too late. Let's get you home," he said.

This marked the recognizing and immediate challenging of dangerous habit number one. We can title this habit "Fuck on the First Date."

In the fifteen minutes from getting the bill to paying the bill to walking to the street corner, I ran through the words in my mouth over and over. *Do you want to come over? Come by? I live around the corner. Wanna come over?* I ran over the sentence without even asking myself, *Are you ready to fuck this stranger yet?*

I was just about to turn toward him and extend the invitation I am very good at extending, when he said, "Can I see you on Friday? But like, early afternoon? I don't wanna wait until the evening."

I quieted the baggage in my head whispering, *Yeah, he wants to see you in the afternoon because he has plans to fuck his way hotter girlfriend in the evening.*

We looked at each other. The neon diner lights dimming while the spattering of 3:00 a.m. weirdos disappeared behind the tension of our goodbye. My peripheral vision mushed into a grey, gelatinous fog as he became my singular point of focus.

He put his arm around me and, without thinking, I sank into the left side of his chest, resting my head on his shoulder like I had done it a hundred times before. He pressed his wet, warm lips against my ear, catching a bit of my hair that had snuck out and pressed against my cheek.

"I'm kind of wowed by you already," he whispered. I sighed in his ear, giving him a tiny peek into how making me feel good sounds. He exhaled hard, then put his hands on my face and kissed just beside my mouth. I let him. Then moved my lips to meet his.

"Friday," he said.

"Friday," I said.

Another word for *test* is *opportunity*. He appeared in my life like an opportunity. An opportunity to really notice the repetitive shit I'd been doing for years.

I clocked bad habit number two during our second date, that Friday afternoon. We can title this bad habit "Don't Tell Him How You Really Feel."

I opened my apartment door, then immediately stepped back, leaning against the door frame to my kitchen. I did this in part because I imagined it would be sexy. Opening the door, allowing him access, then making him move in to get it. But I also did this because I was in the midst of debilitating back spasms and needed the structural support of the door frame.

I had spent the previous few days in bed on heavy-duty painkillers my friend had leftover after getting his wisdom teeth pulled. I had yet to do any sort of research as to what the fuck was happening with my body. I quietly diagnosed it as a tumour that would eventually kill me and moved about my days making peace with my inevitable end.

It wasn't a tumour. Just, backs get bad. And when you've been exercising basically every day since you were sixteen, you get some herniated disks and those disks steal some fun.

We sat on my bed, talking and sweating at each other in the blistering heat until he said, "I'm gonna pounce on you or faint if we don't go for a walk or something."

I smiled, carefully rolled off my bed in secret, excruciating pain, and grabbed my keys.

He clearly knew my neighbourhood far better than I did, so our stroll quickly became a sort of tour as he pointed out where to get the best latte, the best smoothie, the best burnt-caramel-and-black-sea-salt ice cream.

He slipped a perfectly hand-rolled cigarette between his lips. "Let's walk to the observatory. Want to?"

With my back pulsing with barely manageable pain, I said, "Yeah, let's do it."

We walked toward the mountain, passing a handful of dudes he knew, giving me an opportunity to watch his mannerisms remain. Suggesting that the person he was with me was who he was with the rest of the world. A very good sign.

Halfway up the mountain, he said, "I have a little joint in my pocket. Shall we?"

Praying that the joint would dull my spasming back, I said, "Oh my god, yes please."

We reached the top of the mountain and found an incredible perch looking out over Los Angeles at the base of the observatory. Cuddled together in the middle of trees and shrubs and sand that wished it was grass, we lit up and disappeared. I felt his eyes on me. I felt him watching my jaw stretch around my words. I felt him watch my chin bob up and down as I looked at the sky and pointed out a collection of clouds that looked like a pair of scissors.

We made out tucked under the observatory while dozens of tourists took pictures above us, one of whom eventually yelled, "Get a room."

We walked back down the mountain an hour later, subtly sobering up in a way that encouraged my throbbing back pain to rejoin the party. We were five minutes from my place when he suggested walking somewhere else to get something to eat.

At this point, just standing was causing daggers of white-hot pain to shoot up and down my left leg, so I said, "Yeah, I'm hungry. Let's do it."

We strolled back along Hillhurst Avenue. I longingly looked down my street, knowing I was buying myself another couple hours away from my soft surface and that sweet yellow container of cyclobenzaprine.

We sat on the back patio of a little Mexican place. It took me at least three times longer to sit down than it took him, at which point he asked, "Are you in pain?"

I snapped, "I think I'm in a lot of pain actually." I told him about my back and that I thought it was fine and that it perhaps wasn't.

He took me home. And in the following few weeks, he accidentally offered me a unique opportunity to refuse to repeat history.

We were well into the beginning stages of a relationship. I cooked his favourite things and got him saltines and ginger ale when he was sick. We walked around the reservoir and had sleepovers and smoked weed and talked about past lovers.

I went home to Winnipeg for Christmas, hoping my distance wouldn't derail our momentum. We texted regularly over the holidays, and things seemed good until things seemed weird.

Things seemed weird, in fact, because he had gotten someone else pregnant and was in the midst of deciding what to do about it. He told me over FaceTime.

We met up at a café when I got back to L.A. He played with his lentils while telling me that he was going to try to do the right thing, that to him the right thing was committing to her.

As we sat and talked, the existence of his now girlfriend and a possible child sort of dissolved above us, as we remembered how good it felt to be close and we recognized our shared awareness of the fluid nature of invisible rules.

We finished our food and stood up in front of our mangled napkins and empty plates. We hugged. He kissed me on the cheek, and I left.

And as I walked home, I realized I was being given a chance to do things differently. And to my great relief, it was easy. Outside of the uneven power dynamic with Tal, with my feet on the ground, with a community of people who loved me, it was easy to plug my nose and close my eyes and let my brain decide that I was not doing this again.

me

triggers and tools

So, after almost six years signed to Tal, it's fully over.

I could go into detail about the morning we received the
finished paperwork. I could fill you in on how it was raining,
how I like it when it's grey and wet in L.A., how everyone
looks a little lost, everyone looks like they just woke up, tender and tired and a bit swollen. Like the grey forces us all to
face whatever we were running from when we moved here.
Like the dirty sock of a sky is a reminder that wherever we
left still exists.

I could tell you how my phone flirtatiously winked at me, dinging from my bedside table, suggestively requesting my fingers and eyes and attention. How I thought, *Maybe I can prove I am still in control of myself if I count to five before lunging at it.*

How I reached over and pulled its satisfying, sleek body over to me and opened my email to come face to face with Tal's familiar name, written in his familiar signature, finally, begrudgingly releasing me from my deal.

I could tell you how I burst into tears like I was the subject of a perfectly executed surprise party, like I'd walked into a dark room expecting another night of leftover Thai food and tears to find a room filled with every person I have ever truly loved screaming, "Surprise!"

I could tell you all of that, but honestly, he doesn't matter anymore and I don't want to give him one more second of my time. For six years I thought, *It's not quite bad enough yet.* I thought, *Next time. I'll leave next time.* For six years I waited, wading in the shit for the explosive low points to eject me out of the situation. And when I missed an opportunity to depart in the darkness, I sat tight until the next monumental unkindness so that I could ceremoniously leave him, so that my leaving could be an exclamation point and not a smudged ellipsis. And I think maybe I put too much importance on the ceremony of a departure. I never needed any sort of punctuation to go. My unhappiness was punctuation enough.

So, I don't want a ceremony here. I don't want to throw a party or lift a glass of wine. I just want to sit at my kitchen table with a single safety pin; to notice the giant red balloon floating at the door; to stand up, walk over to it, and push the razor-sharp tip through the shining surface. I want to hear it pop, then watch it shrivel and fall to the floor. I want to pick up the limp rubber and toss it into the trash, then make myself lunch. I want to hum while I sloppily peel eggs and mash them up with mayo and pickles and assemble the perfect sandwich.

I met someone new. He's funny and supportive and generous. He compulsively pulls at two chunks of thick black hair that peek out of the sides of his hat, one by each ear. He deliberately leaves them out for the purpose of fondling them. I sit in the passenger seat of his car and watch as he presses the black tendrils against the sides of his face and I'm totally captivated by him. I am captivated by his mouth and cheeks and grubby fingernails. I am captivated by his laugh and how he absolutely has no idea how beautiful he is. His pupils always seem to fill up his entire eye, and when I look at him, I remember that someone once told me our eyes dilate when we're looking at things we like, so I think I'm a thing he likes. He slips his headphones over my ears during scary movies and plays Phoebe Bridgers or The Japanese House or David Bowie and suddenly I am rescued and the stabby screen activity is far less terrifying.

I sketched his face the night we slept together for the first time. I sat on the couch in his hotel room in Ohio and scribbled down his features like I knew them already, like he was mine already. And I feel like I am always with every incarnation of him. I am always with his child self and teen self and adult self, all at once. I feel like he's one of those cut-out things we used to make as kids, where you scissor the shape of a man on folded paper, then pull it open to reveal an entire line of men holding hands in a row. He's so beautiful and so complex, and in falling for someone new, I am facing all of my shit.

And who knows what will happen with us? He is a shining bouquet of red flags and dives in as quickly as he falls out. I'm everything to him as quickly as I am nothing at all.

But suddenly, in looking over my whole life, I'm realizing just how much of this is mine. Just how much of this is of my making, even. Like, we hire the people in our lives who are going to let us live out some shit we haven't handled within ourselves. Like, our most dysfunctional relationships are essentially relationships with the parts of ourselves we haven't quite made peace with yet.

Like, no matter what happens, my shit will be mine and his will be his. And the moves I make will be the direct result of my unique and specific life, and the decisions he makes will be the direct result of his. Like, it's actually kind of impossible for it to be about you, for anything to really be about you, because we are all just digesting each other through these tangled and imperfect screening systems that we build and earn through our entire lives.

And if it ends, it really won't be about me. It won't be my imperfect tummy or the fact that my eyes are absolutely different sizes. It won't be about my relentlessly half-moon-shaped nose and how it is fully trying to escape from one side of my face, because he'll be thinking about his stuff, the reasons he feels unlovable. It'll end because of the lifetime of stuff that lined up to make us see ourselves and each other in specific ways.

And so here I am, fourteen years after losing my virginity, eighteen years after my first kiss, thirteen years after my first major heartbreak, and now I realize that maybe I've been try-ing to learn the same lesson with all these men. And maybe the reason it feels like I've been on a hamster wheel since I was sev-enteen is because I haven't quite learned it yet. I haven't quite figured out how to love myself even when it comes at the cost of losing someone I love. I haven't quite figured out how to pick me. How to pick me in a real way. How to pick me in an if-you-pick-this-you-lose-that kind of way. A picking that has casualties. Necessary casualties.

And yeah, I have learned something big from every man in my life. But more than the specific lessons from specific men, revisiting them all has brutally revealed to me just how much has been shaped by me and my fears and baggage and insecurities.

And now I'm flipping through my memories and I think I'm probably heading to that afternoon when Tal asked if I wanted to sign to him. I'm probably heading to that back alley where Tal casually asked if I was ready to move to L.A. full-time. I'm seeing the memory in slow motion, but I'm not yelling, "Don't sign!" I'm not slowing down at all. I'm watching my past self grin excitedly through the windshield of my mind, and I'm letting it happen. I'm letting five-years-ago me fail to curb her excitement, certain that this is her big break.

And I'm speeding faster now, wondering where I'm heading if not there. Thinking maybe I'm taking myself to any number of desperate nights with Paul or Diego or Daniel. But I'm back at that house party, accepting the beer from Diego's outstretched hand. I'm seeing myself blush a bit and speeding by. I'm not stopping to whisper anything in her ear. I am not stopping to intervene and tell her she can avoid years of pain if she just walks away and talks to someone else.

I'm still speeding.

Maybe I'm going back to when she kissed Paul in the back of that cab. Maybe I'm going back to tell her not to open the letter that followed the kiss, the letter where Paul revealed that he would never love her.

That's not it either.

I'm speeding and speeding, and it's a blur of skin and mouths and tears and cabins and sugar and fluids and injuries and *I love yous*, and over-chlorinated pools. Memories bleeding together like watercolour. Hair and milk and cars and laughing and birthdays and running and homemade friendship bracelets.

And I'm slowing down now. It's my old street. The lights are on inside. It looks like everyone's home. I walk along the path to our front door, to 303. The giant oak trees protecting our house and offering only slivers of silvery light on the faded pink sidewalk chalk.

I turn my key and leave the stack of mail outside; my dad will get it later. I walk into the foyer.

Standing under the yellow chandelier, I listen to my sisters eating breakfast with my mom in the kitchen, sitting around the busted countertop, beside where the original back door was before the renovations.

My dad is coming up the basement stairs with a bag of raisins and a bag of carrots. He's humming a song I know. I bet he's about to make lunches.

I catch a glimpse of my mom's flowing black hair as I turn away to take the long staircase upstairs, skipping the creaking step third from the top, the one I didn't place weight on for ten years.

I come to the landing at the top of the stairs. I can hear my brother, Damien, thumping around on the third floor above me, the muted sounds of Marilyn Manson playing on the other side of the carpeted floor.

I realize I'm looking for fourteen-year-old me; I'm looking for fourteen-year-old her. I walk into my old bedroom. The room beside the bathroom with its folding-out mirrors that allowed her to see and judge and hate all sides of her body at once. I see her lying on her back, her hands over her soft, imperfect tummy. I see her deciding to do whatever it takes to get a man to love her. Even if it means not being her at all. Even if it means hiding her anger and her drama and her needs.

She is looking up at her ceiling, thinking, *No one's ever gonna love me. No one's ever gonna touch or kiss or hold me.*

And I think I know why I'm stopped here. I'm stopped because I finally have something to tell her. Something true. Something I actually mean. I'm stopped here because I realize I'm happy. And being happy means making peace with every single tiny decision that brought me here. I have to accept everything that came before, because every single turn and kiss and broken heart and missed flight and fight and red light brought me to this exact moment. And changing anything at all, leaning down to pick up any piece of trash, skipping any single party or dinner or coffee or conversation, would change the entire course of my life. And I like my life. And I am happy.

I lie down beside her and take one of her hands off her soft, imperfect tummy. I press her palm to my lips and kiss it.

Then lowering our arms, I intertwine my fingers with hers.

As we lay side by side, I whisper, "Do it again, exactly the same, for the first time. I love you."

acknowledgements

I would like to thank the following superheroes:

My agent, Jessica Alvarez, for taking a chance on me. This book would not be this book without you.

Kathryn Lane and Rachel Spence, for saying yes. This has been a life-changing process for me, and I am deeply grateful to you both. To Elena Radic, Barbara Bower, Laura Boyle, Lisa Marie Smith, and the entire Dundurn team for supporting my vision and handling my assertive passion with so much patience, grace, and kindness.

Susan Fitzgerald. Thank you for letting me keep my sentence fragments.

Hernan. Thank you for being the first editor of this book. And thank you for encouraging me to keep the process of writing it insulated and private the many times I felt like posting snippets, with a peace sign and my tongue out, under a freckle filter on an Instagram story.

Dad. Mom. There is no way I could have written any of this without the absolute confidence that you would still love me on the other side. I am way luckier than any one person has any right to be. Thank you for my life.

Kendra, Danica, Damien: my siblings, my soulmates. There is nothing we could do to lose each other's love, and that has offered me an essentially risk-free existence. Yes, I wrote graphic details about my life, and yet I have literally nothing to lose. Thank you.

Jacqueline. Thank you for being the big sister I never had.

Rae. Thank you for becoming family.

Lou, for offering me a home at a few critical points in my life and for being my godmother, teacher, friend.

My unbelievably patient friends who have never written me off as a complete lost cause the many times I was hell-bent on destroying myself. Thank you for sticking it out and not making me feel stupid for making the same mistakes over and over.

Marc, for seeing me through nearly two decades of heartbreaks and general self-loathing. And for writing me the most supportive, magical email of all time, from which I have poached a line or two for the back of this very book. Thank you.

Maytav and Lulu. The first badass women to change my life in Los Angeles. I am eternally grateful.

Taylor, Alex, Bonj, Anna, Mary, Rotana, Clara, Ally, Ben, Wafia, Charlotte and the life-changers that are the Lawrences, Dayle, Hale, Leila, Jane, Liza, Dan, James, Kaia, Cindy, Lena, and all the other friends and supporters who will continue loving me on the other side of this publication.

And to all the men in this book, sincerely, thank you for not marrying me. I would have said yes to any one of you, and I am so glad I didn't. I am profoundly grateful for all the lessons my pain and experience have taught me.

Many names and identifying characteristics in *People You Follow* have been changed to protect those involved.